One Brain Cell Left

Inside a Classic Rock and Roll Journalist's
Storied Vault

Rosy Steve Rosenthal

DEDICATION

For my amazing wife, Marla, my editor and support system, who has loved me and believed in me for more than 30 years, even when I stopped loving and believing in myself;

and

For Landon and Torrey, whose unconditional love inspired this unconventional father to document his unconventional life.

Contents

Chapter 1

I'm completely unknown worldwide

My life by the numbers:

(1) The number of brain cells I have left.

(12) The number of years that I spent as a rock and roll
interviewer in order to achieve No. 1 above.

(85) The number of inductees into the Rock and Roll Hall of
Fame that I interviewed.

(174) The number of recording artists that I interviewed who
had at least one No. 1 hit.

(348) The number of No. 1 songs recorded by those 174
artists.

My interviews were heard daily on radio stations around the
globe during much of the late '70s and '80s. They were aired in every
radio market in the US.

And yet, I'm completely unknown worldwide.

I've interviewed Grammy winners for Pop, Rock, R&B, Country,
Rap, Jazz, Alternative, Disco, Metal, Reggae and Comedy.

I've interviewed Academy Award winners for Best Actor, Best Actress, Best Supporting Actor and Best Supporting Actress.

I've interviewed Hall of Famers in baseball, football, basketball, hockey, golf, boxing, motorcycle racing and drag racing. In fact, I've interviewed inductees into 24 nationally recognized Halls of Fame.

Still, I'm completely unknown worldwide.

****

I interviewed Paul McCartney backstage in Miami, where his late wife, Linda, gave me a holistic remedy to treat my terrible cold.

I interviewed Madonna when she was first starting out. She told me exactly how big she was going to be. I left the interview unconvinced.

The four most boring people I ever interviewed were Michael Jackson, Janet Jackson, Harrison Ford and Sean Connery.

I've commiserated with Tina Turner and Phil Collins about each of our divorces.

I first interviewed John Mellencamp when he was still known by most as Johnny Cougar. His infidelity led us to share very awkward moments on two separate occasions.

I pulled the plug on interviews with Stevie Nicks and Billy Idol when they were incoherent ... whacked out of their minds.

My first words to Lionel Richie were, "So they tell me you've become a real asshole since you've gotten all this success." We both laughed.

I traveled behind the Iron Curtain in Hungary as a guest of the German band, Scorpions ... and with the Monsters of Rock tour in Germany that featured Ozzy Osbourne and an up-and-coming Bon Jovi.

One Brain Cell Left

I waited more than an hour for Alice Cooper to show up for an afternoon interview. He arrived with Elton John's co-writer, Bernie Taupin, who was very drunk and ruined the interview.

I change the radio station every time I hear a Hall & Oates song. They treated me fine, but as soon as the interview ended, they treated their staff like shit right in front of me.

When I was 30 pounds lighter with long, curly hair and a tight butt, Dolly Parton made a very approving sound and started flirting with me as I walked through the door.

Little Richard smiled at me and told me he liked Jewish boys. I was flattered.

Randy Jones, the cowboy in the Village People, checked me out up and down ... and grinned.

An African-American recording artist told me he wanted me to be his "White Meat" ... on multiple occasions.

Poor Joe Cocker. When I interviewed him, he had no idea what year it was.

I sat next to George Harrison at a press conference and found him to be completely down-to-earth.

Unfortunately, I can't say the same about Ringo.

Patti LaBelle cried on two different instances when she was alone with me.

I interviewed Whitney Houston just two weeks after her first album was released, and she was already a diva. It came naturally. Whitney's cousin, Dionne Warwick, was an unpleasant diva long before Whitney was born.

I interviewed Mr. Las Vegas, Wayne Newton, in the comfort of his dressing room between shows. He was the first person I ever met who wore contact lenses through the night. He hadn't taken them out in three months.

When I interviewed Gene Simmons, he was very impressed by the length of my tongue.

Rosy Steve Rosenthal

I first interviewed Arnold Schwarzenegger when he knew about four words of English. His heavy Austrian accent and extremely limited English vocabulary made the interview completely unusable for radio.

I interviewed Spinal Tap, Indiana Jones, James Bond, Morticia Addams, the Scarecrow, Marty McFly, Lenny & Squiggy, Wonder Woman, Ned Flanders, Peg Bundy, Eddie Munster, Venus Flytrap, Potsie Weber, Arnold Horshack and the man who uttered the most important movie line of all-time ... "Bueller?" ... "Bueller?" ... "Bueller?"

The Jamaican government provided me with a private tour of the island nation following the fall of the Marxist regime there.

I interviewed the winner of an international marlin fishing tournament in Port Antonio, Jamaica ... with his drunken cougar wife hitting on me right in front of him. She reminded me of Dean Wormer's wife from *Animal House*.

Jamaican recording artist, Peter Tosh, smoked the largest spliff I've ever seen. It was the size of a cotton-candy paper cone ... something out of a Cheech & Chong movie.

I've been stoned at New York's Madison Square Garden and embarrassingly drunk at a Hollywood party for the group Bad Company.

Mel Brooks ran after me.

Mickey Mantle swore at me.

Kareem Abdul-Jabbar intentionally treated me like shit in the Laker locker room in front of dozens of people. Asshole.

A Hall of Fame major league umpire flipped me off in front of thousands of oohing and aahing fans at Dodger Stadium. I could be an asshole, too.

Willie Mays nearly broke my hand ... with a line drive.

I chatted with Yogi Berra in the Yankee clubhouse during the World Series.

One Brain Cell Left

I showered in the Los Angeles Lakers locker room, the same one that Wilt Chamberlain and teammates used. Not surprisingly, it had the tallest shower heads I've ever seen.

I had man crushes on Joe Namath and Smokey Robinson when I interviewed them.

I played a college ice hockey game against UCLA on the former home ice of the Los Angeles Kings, the Fabulous Forum.

In 1974, my Co-Editor-in-Chief and I did something that even *Playboy's* Hugh Hefner never had the balls to do. We ran full frontal nudity on the cover of the college newspaper.

Apple co-founder Steve Wozniak flew to LA in his private jet just to do an interview with me about the US Festival and immediately flew back home.

Supreme Court Justice William O. Douglas once called me with his Christmas wishes.

I talked at length with a woman who survived the atomic bomb at Hiroshima.

I conducted the last interview ever granted by the most famous American spy pilot of the 20th Century ... before he died in a mysterious helicopter crash.

I peered through the window into the Unabomber's cabin ... when no one was allowed to see it.

I talked at length with Charles Manson's bumbling attorney, and with Vince Bugliosi, author of *Helter Skelter* and Manson's chief prosecutor.

I found Robert Kennedy assassin Sirhan Sirhan's mother in the phone book and gave her a call.

I had a cop's gun pressed against my forehead in my own living room. The search warrant was for a machine gun and explosives.

I had a gun pulled on me at one of the radio stations where I was a DJ ... by the station owner himself.

Rosy Steve Rosenthal

I was once commanded to leave a town … because I was living with a woman outside of marriage. It was Wyoming. 1976. Pickup trucks with gun racks. I willingly left town … and obediently never returned.

I once had a conversation with two friends in Michigan and realized I was the only one of us who hadn't been shot in Detroit.

Someone tried to kill me by attempting to run me off the freeway within hours after my son's birth.

I was almost killed three days before that, when a defective Firestone tire exploded on my Corvette at high speed in the Nevada desert. One month later, Firestone recalled more than seven million of the tires, after they were found responsible for the deaths of dozens of people.

I've saved a life on two separate occasions … one human, one canine.

I once stepped out of my front door … only to be met by a bear seven feet away from me.

I threw a pit bull off a cliff when he was trying to kill my two dogs. He survived, but man was he dazed.

I received a hate-crime death threat during one of my radio shifts, because I was Jewish.

One year I asked my parents for an electric piano for Hanukkah and got an electric blanket instead.

During the 1967 Summer of Love, I went to a hippie love-in at the iconic Griffith Park carousel in LA. I was 14 years old. I had to take two buses to get there.

A few months later, my left eye was on *Days of Our Lives* for several minutes during a courtroom scene. I was taking the NBC Studios tour in Burbank, when the producers asked me to sit in on the jury. I was 14, looked 12 and was wearing shorts in the jury box.

I wrote 666 in felt pen on my six-week-old son's bald head … just to hear my ex-wife shriek when she saw it.

One Brain Cell Left

I got high on hash after my mother-in-law's funeral and got the uncontrollable laughs.

I was a male model … for one hour.

I married my sister-in-law … to her second husband. The State of California and the County of Riverside appointed me as an officiant for one day so that I could perform the ceremony.

My second wife, Marla, and I were married in a mountain hideaway where gangster Bugsy Siegel once ran an illegal gaming hall, brothel and bootleg operation. It just seemed like the perfect place for us.

After Marla decided we would get married on a Saturday in May, I picked May 16th. Twenty minutes later I confessed that it was the anniversary of my first marriage, so I couldn't forget it. Needless to say, we changed the date.

The rabbi who married us was stoned at the time.

I was married in a shirt that was worn by Jimmy Stewart in one of his Western Movies.

On multiple occasions I've asked Marla if it would be okay for me to bring a date to her funeral.

I've been an outspoken supporter of same-sex marriage since I produced a radio talk show on the subject in 1975.

I was invited to Dr. Demento's wedding, but I had sex instead.

****

And through it all, I've remained completely unknown worldwide.

My life hasn't always been pretty, but it's made for a lot of interesting stories. And I've got the brain cell to prove it.

Chapter 2

I found my past hanging on a museum wall

I can't always paint a pretty picture of the superstars I've interviewed. Some have been absolute sweethearts; others have been absolute assholes. And they're not always the ones you'd expect.

I'm never asked what I talked about with celebrities. People only want to know what the stars were like in person. It was the common denominator once I started my rock and roll career as a 25-year-old journalist in 1978.

This book answers the "What were they like?" questions about a cross-section of superstar entertainers, newsmakers and athletes that I interviewed. But it's equally about the unique and unusual life that I've led outside the entertainment industry.

I was never comfortable with the idea of looking back over my life. When I left the radio and entertainment industries, I left completely. May 22, 1990. About the only time I'd feel even a little nostalgic was when I'd see one of the old K-tel record commercials on TV. I'd interviewed so many of the artists.

My wife, Marla, and a collection of friends and family had been after me for three decades to compile all of my unusual and unique stories. Because of severe bipolar disorder, it took 20 years before I could face documenting my life. I'm not even sure how I finally made the breakthrough. But in November 2010, while vacationing on the north shore of Oahu, I just started typing and didn't stop until I'd written down more than 100 very unique things that I'd experienced.

I had no idea what I would do with them, but every few months, I'd add to the list.

Three years after I'd started taking down notes, Marla and I moved to Michigan. A walk through the prestigious Detroit Historical Museum would provide the impetus for this book. Prominently displayed on the wall of the museum's *Kid Rock Music Lab* was a *Billboard* magazine Hot 100 chart from September 1980. I'd interviewed 58 of the 100.

That really jolted me. Since I'd left behind that part of my life so many years before, I had no idea of the breadth of my work. For the first time, I was actually proud of the career that I'd downplayed for 35 years. It was hanging on a museum wall right in front of me.

I conducted more than 1600 interviews before bipolar disorder took full control. It was truly a life of sexual harassment, drugs, more sexual harassment, more drugs and rock and roll. Writing this book is the exclamation point on one wild rollercoaster ride.

Chapter 3

I *REALLY* didn't want to like Paul McCartney

The Beatles in 1964. Paul McCartney is second from left

Credit: United Press International

By the time spring had sprung in 1990, I was done. My heart was no longer in it. I'd been in syndicated radio for 13 years. I'd spent the last nine-and-a-half as Director of Artist Relations with the Westwood One Radio Networks, the largest producer of radio programs in the world. It was time to move on.

I'd been working on my own sports marketing project, and that's where my head was. The thrill of doing another music interview just wasn't there. So when Paul McCartney's people called me to set up an interview in Miami, I decided I'd assign it to one of my reporters. I wasn't interested in flying cross-country, then flying back to LAX the next day.

Then the backlash hit. First, Marla said I HAD to do it ... it was McCARTNEY. Then Marla's cousin, Jeff, started in. Jeff's a lifelong Beatles fan and a professor of classical guitar at Chapman University in Orange, California. Even he was in awe of McCartney.

More of the same from friends and family. "He's a BEATLE. It's illegal in 32 states to turn down an interview with a Beatle."

And so, I was shamed into interviewing Paul McCartney.

****

April 15, 1990

I drive straight to my hotel from the Miami airport. I could use the rest. I caught a cold yesterday doing an interview in Memphis, and I feel awful.

I have a lot of time to kill ... the interview won't take place for hours. I'll have him all to myself; I'll be the only journalist there. We're scheduled to do it backstage before his concert tonight at Joe Robbie Stadium. He's still so popular, he can fill a football stadium.

But there's a problem. It's an outdoor concert, and there's a torrential rain. I mean torrential. South Florida torrential. I call McCartney's office in New York to see if the concert's been canceled, but it's Sunday. I get the machine.

Crap. I fly all the way to Miami, and I have no idea if the interview's even happening. Hours go by and no let-up in the weather. This is before cell phones, email, texting. If I leave the hotel, they'll have no way of contacting me. If they want to move the interview someplace else, I'm screwed.

Finally, I have no choice but to drive out to the stadium.

It's an unbelievable downpour. I'm on I-95, and it's monsoonal outside. I'm scared shitless. What should've taken 20 minutes takes an hour. I get there. Frazzled. But I get there.

I pull into the stadium parking lot, and the rain stops. A good omen. There are actually a fair amount of cars already parked. The attendant directs me into a spot on the grass. I take one step out of the car, and I slurp into the mud, down to my ankle. I have to laugh at the absurdity. Who puts a grass parking lot at a South Florida stadium?

****

They're expecting me. I'm ushered into the bowels of the venue. The weather's made my cold even worse. I'm a sorry sight when I meet him.

I've flown cross-country against my wishes, caught a terrible cold, drove through a god-awful downpour, slurped through the mud. And now I'm face-to-face with the man who's made me do it. I REALLY don't want to like him.

But he's totally disarmed me. Welcoming. Down-to-earth just like George Harrison had been at the press conference 11 years ago. It's impossible to dislike him. The chip's knocked off my shoulder. I'm talking with HIM!

I tell him we'll talk about his latest project, the *Flowers in the Dirt* LP, for about 20 minutes and then transition into Beatles stuff. I'd told Ringo the same thing years before. The only problem was, when I brought up the Beatles, Ringo began to whisper his answers. It was his way of saying, "We'll talk about the Beatles, but you won't be able to hear it."

But Paul's different. He's actually happy to talk about his past. He tells me his current tour's the first time he can actually hear himself playing some of the Beatles songs. No screaming fans. Just appreciative ones. He's truly enjoying touring and playing live.

I'm suffering. It's impossible to hide my cold. Compassionately, Paul says when the interview's over, he wants to take me to his wife, Linda, for her to prescribe some holistic cold remedies. Minutes later he does just that. He tells Linda that I'm really sick. She takes it from there. Like Paul, she's a delight. "You need to take this root and these berries." I have no idea what she's talking about. I just nod and smile. She couldn't be more concerned. Somehow now my cold doesn't feel so bad.

****

It turns out to be a beautiful night. The weather's cleared, and the crowd's anticipation is electric. The stadium erupts when he comes on stage. It's been 26 years since *The Ed Sullivan Show*. The young teens of 1964 have brought their young teens to experience it together.

And what a thrill it is for me. Thirty minutes before, I'd been talking with the man who's now such a commanding presence on stage. Paul had been right. You can hear every word, every note. He's having the time of his life. So are tens of thousands of Beatles and McCartney fans. Generations singing along together.

And that was it. A month later my interview career was over. Marla had shamed me into doing the interview. Now I was thrilled that she'd made me do it. It was the perfect way to go out. Thirteen years and 1600 interviews. I wouldn't look back for more than 20 years.

Chapter 4

174 artists that I interviewed who had at least one No. 1 hit

Whitney Houston had 11 No. 1 songs.
Credit: PH2 Mark Kettenhofen

These artists recorded a total of 348 No. 1 songs.
(Number of No. 1 hits in parentheses)

ABBA (1)
Aerosmith (1)
Air Supply (1)
Herb Alpert (2)
America (2)
The Animals (1)
The Association (2)
Atlantic Starr (1)
Patti Austin (1)
Average White Band (1)
Toni Basil (1)
Bay City Rollers (1)
The Beach Boys (4)
The Beatles (20)
The Bee Gees (9)
The Bellamy Brothers (1)
Berlin (1)
Blondie (4)
Gary U.S. Bonds (1)
Bread (1)
Bobby Brown (2)
Peabo Bryson (1)
Glen Campbell (2)
Captain & Tennille (2)
Irene Cara (1)
Belinda Carlisle (1)
Kim Carnes (1)
The Carpenters (3)
Peter Cetera (2)
Harry Chapin (1)
Chubby Checker (2)

One Brain Cell Left

Chic (2)
Chicago (3)
The Chi-Lites (1)
Joe Cocker (1)
Phil Collins (7)
The Commodores (2)
Culture Club (1)
Billy Davis, Jr. (1)
Kiki Dee (1)
Def Leppard (1)
Dexys Midnight Runners (1)
Donovan (1)
The Doobie Brothers (2)
The Doors (2)
Duran Duran (2)
Earth, Wind & Fire (1)
Sheena Easton (1)
Yvonne Elliman (1)
The Emotions (1)
Exile (1)
The Fifth Dimension (2)
Roberta Flack (3)
Fleetwood Mac (1)
Foreigner (1)
The Four Seasons (5)
The Four Tops (2)
Peter Gabriel (1)
Gloria Gaynor (1)
Genesis (1)
Grand Funk Railroad (2)
The Guess Who (1)
Daryl Hall and John Oates (6)
Isaac Hayes (1)

Herman's Hermits (2)

Thelma Houston (1)

Whitney Houston (11)

The Human League (2)

Billy Idol (1)

James Ingram (2)

INXS (1)

Janet Jackson (10)

Michael Jackson (13)

The Jackson 5 (4)

Jan & Dean (1)

Joan Jett and the Blackhearts (1)

Robert John (1)

KC and the Sunshine Band (5)

Eddie Kendricks (1)

The Knack (1)

Gladys Knight & the Pips (1)

Kool and the Gang (1)

Labelle (1)

Patti LaBelle (1)

Cyndi Lauper (2)

Gary Lewis & the Playboys (1)

Huey Lewis and the News (3)

Gordon Lightfoot (1)

Lipps, Inc. (1)

Kenny Loggins (1)

Los Lobos (1)

The Love Unlimited Orchestra (1)

Lulu (1)

Madonna (12)

Henry Mancini (1)

Manfred Mann (2)

The Manhattans (1)

One Brain Cell Left

Johnny Mathis (2)
Paul McCartney (3)
Marilyn McCoo (1)
Michael McDonald (1)
Maureen McGovern (1)
Don McLean (1)
Glenn Medeiros (1)
Bill Medley (1)
John Mellencamp (1)
Men at Work (2)
The Miracles (2)
The Monkees (3)
Anne Murray (1)
Johnny Nash (1)
Ricky Nelson (2)
Olivia Newton-John (5)
Billy Ocean (3)
The Ohio Players (2)
The O'Jays (1)
The Osmonds (1)
Robert Palmer (1)
Ray Parker, Jr. (1)
Dolly Parton (2)
Peaches & Herb (1)
Peter and Gordon (1)
Peter, Paul and Mary (1)
Player (1)
The Police (1)
Billy Preston (2)
Eddie Rabbitt (1)
The Raiders (1)
Helen Reddy (3)
REO Speedwagon (2)

Rosy Steve Rosenthal

Lionel Richie (5)
The Righteous Brothers (2)
Minnie Riperton (1)
Johnny Rivers (1)
Tommy Roe (2)
Kenny Rogers (2)
Rose Royce (1)
The Spinners (1)
Rick Springfield (1)
The Staple Singers (2)
Edwin Starr (1)
Ringo Starr (2)
Starship (3)
Ray Stevens (2)
Amii Stewart (1)
Sting (1)
Styx (1)
Survivor (1)
Billy Swan (1)
The Sylvers (1)
A Taste of Honey (1)
Johnnie Taylor (1)
Tears for Fears (2)
The Temptations (4)
The Three Degrees (1)
Toto (1)
Tina Turner (1)
UB40 (2)
USA for Africa (1)
U2 (2)
Frankie Valli (2)
Billy Vera & the Beaters (1)
John Waite (1)

One Brain Cell Left

Jennifer Warnes (2)
Dionne Warwick (2)
Mary Wells (1)
Barry White (1)
Whitesnake (1)
Deniece Williams (2)
Vanessa Williams (1)
Wings (6)
Steve Winwood (2)
Bill Withers (1)
Yes (1)

Chapter 5

Speak up, Michael. You're killing me.

Credit: Casta03/Wikimedia Commons

I'm often asked who my worst interview subject was, and the answer may surprise you. First, a qualifier. The worst was not the assholiest.

A print journalist can take a one-word answer and turn it into a thousand words. For a radio journalist, a one-word answer is death.

Enter The Jacksons.

****

December 12, 1978

The Jackson 5 are still trying to bounce back from a bitter, much-publicized break-up from Motown, where they've literally grown up from childhood. Due to a legal battle, they're now known simply as The Jacksons. The release of their third Epic Records LP in two years, *Destiny*, is just five days away.

I've only been doing music interviews for two months, so to get an interview with The Jacksons is a big score for me. I've been a fan since their debut album, *Diana Ross Presents the Jackson 5*, spawned four straight No. 1 hits in 1969-70.

I confidently enter the conference room at CBS Records in Century City. All five are waiting for me. Missing is Jermaine, who's stayed behind as a solo artist at Motown after marrying company founder Berry Gordy's daughter, Hazel. I'll interview him in a few years. Youngest brother Randy has stepped in to replace him.

I only have a split-second to size up the situation. My agenda is to ask one or two questions of each of the Jackson 4, then zero in on the real prize, the now 21-year-old Michael.

Tito, Marlon and Jackie are easy interviews. Randy's so intimidated being interviewed that he's not worth my time. I quickly move passed him. Michael is mine.

He isn't yet the "King of Pop," but he's still Michael Jackson, a superstar before his testicles had dropped. He's no longer a teen idol; he's grown into an adult. And he's heading into the studio to record a solo album in his first collaboration with legendary producer Quincy Jones … a combination that will yield the smash *Off the Wall* LP. I want the interview in the can when it's released. I'm ready to squeeze a thousand questions into a half hour.

I quickly go from excited to puzzled to frustrated to sad in the span of one minute. The star entertainer, who's mesmerized millions on stage, screen and records, is scared to death, shy beyond belief. He can't string together two audible words. Speak up, Michael. You're killing me.

I try a few different approaches … all with the same result: absolutely unusable. It's sad to see him struggle with even the simplest questions. I'm embarrassed for him. He's the worst interviewee I've ever met.

Chapter 6

So why am I unknown worldwide?

Yes, I was an on-the-air disk jockey, sports play-by-play announcer and news director at various radio stations. And, yes, for years my interviews were heard all over the world. But for the last 12 years of my radio career, my voice and the questions that I asked the celebrities were edited out of what you heard, and the voice of each program's host was edited in. The host would say, "And Whitney said, "…..." and then you'd hear Whitney Houston's response. It made it seem as if the host had conducted the actual interview. My voice was edited out of thousands of programs on hundreds and hundreds of radio stations. So, yes, my interviews were heard all over the world, but I wasn't. I remain completely unknown worldwide.

I have no complaints; I traded my ego for money. The pay was good, and I'd burned out waking up every morning in the three o'clock hour to open a radio station at five. I didn't miss being on-the-air, except for baseball and basketball play-by-play. That was my forte, and not continuing that career path was one of my main regrets.

But I fell into doing entertainment interviews. It was an easy way to earn a living, paid the bills and bought Marla and me a modest home in the mountains of the San Bernardino National Forest. I'm fortunate to wake up every morning surrounded by 100-foot cedars and pines with a creek running through my backyard … just incredible natural beauty. And that suits me much better than my years in the city.

Although audiences didn't know me, I was known by pretty much every music industry publicist in LA and many in New York and Nashville. And most knew me simply by my nickname, Rosy. There were eight other Steves at Westwood One, and I'd been Rosy since I was 10 years old, so it just made sense to go by my nickname. Besides, I usually wore softball jerseys to the interviews, and all of the shirts had "Rosy" typed across the back. Many in the music industry had no idea that Rosy wasn't my real name.

Many people who knew me were envious of my job and my access to celebrities, but I was pretty blasé about it. I knew my work was different from most, but, with rare exceptions, I didn't put the stars on a pedestal. That allowed me to excel in the interviews. I felt I was the celebrities' equal, and they usually picked up on it, so I was treated with respect by most.

There were perks, too. My hours were my own, and I came and went as I pleased. I'd get to the office around 10:00 or 11:00 a.m., work a half hour to an hour on the phone setting up interviews, then go for a two-margarita lunch. I'd do an interview or two in the afternoon and call it a day.

I was invited to every rock concert and movie screening in LA, eight nights a week (which was a boost to my dating life), but even that got old. I turned down hundreds of industry functions, even the Grammys, which I assigned to my reporters to cover.

I grew my hair long and curly and wore jeans and Nikes everyday to go with my softball jerseys. I was able to travel to New York, Nashville, wherever there was an entertainment tie-in, when I wanted, staying in the best hotels, all expenses paid.

One Brain Cell Left

Plus, I got every album release free from every major record label for more than a decade. The post office had to give me the largest PO Box they had just to handle all of the record albums that I received on a daily basis. And a liberal expense account allowed me to take music-, movie- and book-industry friends to lunch and dinner at nicer restaurants. Not a bad gig. It's amazing how delicious scampi tastes at noon when the company's paying for it.

Rosy Steve Rosenthal

Chapter 7

Madonna: Queen Shit with a muffin-top

Credit: Olavtenbroek/Wikimedia Commons

One Brain Cell Left

December 14, 1983

I misjudged her. I misread her. I underestimated her. To say the very least. I was never more wrong about a new artist than I was about Madonna.

****

It's Christmas time 1983. For the past three months, I've been following the rise up the charts of her single, "Holiday." The song is getting lots of airplay on Urban Contemporary stations, and I need her for Westwood One's R&B show, *The Countdown*. Like many at the time, and before she hit MTV, I assume she's African-American.

When I arrive for the interview, it's obvious I'm mistaken.

Colorful Christmas decorations belie how dreary it is outside. I meet her in a small office at Warner Bros. Records in Burbank. She seems strangely out of place wearing a bare-midriff top in December. Her muffin-top dangles loosely over her jeans. Not a good look. Not a good first impression.

I try every which way to engage her, but she's not very interested. She's incredibly aloof, especially for a new artist. She needs me more than I need her. I can deliver airplay to millions of listeners, but she couldn't care less. She's not scoring points with me.

It nosedives from there. She has absolutely no humility. She tells me exactly how big she's gonna be. Not just a star. Not just a superstar. But a Mega-Star. She portrays herself as a sex symbol. She better lose the muffin-top first.

I've interviewed many performers who were conceited, but this young woman is the most arrogant I've ever come across. It's her first single to enter *Billboard's* Hot 100. She's barely cracked the Top 20 on the charts, and she's acting like she's Queen Shit. Like I've seen with so many artists before her, I'm thinking that her arrogance will kill her career before it ever gets started. I can't wait for the interview to end.

****

Years later, I would read that her producer, then boyfriend, "Jellybean" Benitez admitted that "she could be a bitch." At least I know it wasn't just me.

There's a fine line between belief in oneself and conceit. I still think she crossed the line. But I give her credit. She was obviously right all along.

And the muffin-top ... well let's just say, she lost it and I gained it. It looks worse on me than it did on her.

Chapter 8

Record Report: How it all began

October 12, 1978

In 1978, I owned a small recording studio in Van Nuys, California, which I'd purchased the year before to produce my national radio programs. In the spring of '78, I got a call from a guy looking for a studio to do preproduction for a syndicated radio show he owned called *Record Report*. Robert W. Morgan, a Los Angeles disk jockey that I'd listened to for years, was host of the show. It turned out that the show's owner was a high school classmate of mine named Gary. I was happy for the work.

Six months after I started doing *Record Report*'s preproduction, Gary asked me if I knew anyone who could do rock and roll interviews. His reporter had burned a hole through her nose doing tons of cocaine, and he needed someone ASAP. He thought I might know somebody. I told him I didn't, but I'd be happy to help out doing interviews while he looked for a replacement. Apparently he didn't look very hard, because after my first few interviews, he asked me to stay on permanently. And that's how I fell into my rock and roll career. I didn't seek it out; it found me. People ask me how to break into doing music interviews. I tell them I have no idea. It was handed to me on a silver platter.

I wasn't even that big of a music fan. I was a news and sports guy. I'd always looked down on entertainment journalists. Now I was one.

31

Rosy Steve Rosenthal

My rock and roll interview career began on Columbus Day, October 12, 1978. My first music interview was with Ronnie Hammond, lead singer of the Atlanta Rhythm Section, whose hits included "So Into You" and "Imaginary Lover."

In the first month alone, I interviewed Foreigner, Isaac Hayes, Styx, 10cc, KC & the Sunshine Band, Dr. John, Toto, Chaka Khan, the Grass Roots, Wonder Woman Lynda Carter, Arlo Guthrie and more than a dozen others. It was trial by fire. Before the end of the year, I'd added such diverse entertainers as Michael Jackson, Alice Cooper, Tanya Tucker, the Fifth Dimension, Yes, Sha Na Na, the Bay City Rollers, Black Sabbath, Village People, Moody Blues, Wayne Newton, Glen Campbell, Steppenwolf, Grateful Dead and Dick Clark. I've got to believe that's the only time all of those celebrities were ever mentioned in the same sentence.

My true indoctrination came just 12 days after my first interview. I'd been used to wearing pullover sweaters, slacks, dress shirts, dress shoes and short-cropped hair. That's the way I showed up for my interview with Foreigner at Atlantic Records. I sat patiently in the lobby waiting to be called in, ignored by everybody in the office. Then a man sat down next to me in a dirty T-shirt with a pack of cigarettes rolled up in his sleeve. It looked as if he hadn't bathed in a while ... his hair was all matted down. It turned out he was an LA and nationally syndicated disk jockey named Jim Ladd. Despite his appearance, the Atlantic Records women were fawning over him like he was a god. One after another came by to pay homage to this homeless-looking guy. I knew then that I needed a complete makeover. From that day forward I let my hair grow into a huge Jew-fro and dressed in jeans, sneakers and softball jerseys.

And it worked. Suddenly I fit in. In less than three months, I was known by every record company in Los Angeles. Despite my protestations, somehow I'd become an entertainment journalist. It was all a mistake. I was just trying to help out a high school classmate.

****

One Brain Cell Left

I conducted more than 350 interviews in the 13 months from October 1978 through November 1979, when it became apparent that *Record Report* was having financial difficulties. Still, even after they missed my paycheck, I continued doing interviews for them.

****

November 20, 1979

On Monday, November 19, 1979, I interviewed a very unglamorous newcomer named Pat Benatar at Chrysalis Records on the western edge of the Sunset Strip. Her first charting single, "Heartbreaker," was released just three weeks before. She was wearing a braless tank top … her little tits barely making a dent in the fabric. Her unkempt hair looked like it hadn't been washed in days. Nothing to portend the patented Benatar look that would be satirized in the movie *Fast Times at Ridgemont High* just a couple of years later. None of the Aqua Net hair, the multi-colored eye shadow, the leg warmers. Nothing to indicate she was a rock star in waiting.

The next day, I drove over to Warner Bros. Records in Burbank, where I interviewed Nicolette Larson. Her "Lotta Love" single had made its way into *Billboard's* Top 10 earlier in the year. I was excited to get her, and I wasn't disappointed. She was warm and welcoming, no ego whatsoever. It turned out to be the last interview I would ever do for *Record Report*.

When they missed my paycheck a second time, I was done. I was only going to do interviews for them for a few weeks until they found someone permanently, and it turned into a year. I was burned out on rock and roll. It wasn't something I craved. I knew I'd done my very last rock and roll interview. Or so I thought.

Chapter 9

Westwood One: A decade of debauchery

November 3, 1980

A year after I quit *Record Report* and the music industry, I got a call from a friend, Lynnsey Guerrero, who was the company's former producer. A few months after we left *Record Report* a day apart, Lynnsey became a producer at the Westwood One Radio Networks. The nature of his call was unexpected. He wanted me to come to work for Westwood One to conduct their interviews. They had just fired their interviewer and needed someone to fill the role. He asked me to meet with Norm Pattiz, the owner.

I told him I wasn't interested in doing any more rock and roll interviews, and I wasn't interested in returning to syndicated radio. I had just left an unpleasant situation as one of the editors at the *Los Angeles Herald-Examiner* and intended to take some time off to determine my next career move. But Lynnsey was persistent. Still, I wouldn't budge. Then Lynnsey said something that changed my life forever. "Don't burn your bridges ... meet with Norm. You never know when you'll need him." That made a lot of sense. I could meet with Norm and tell him that the timing wasn't right ... but still leave the door open for future work, if and when I needed it.

One Brain Cell Left

About a month later, I found myself in Norm's office in a very hip building in Culver City, just a block from MGM's legendary movie studios. At *Record Report*, Lynnsey and I shared a dingy office with old, dirty carpet and only one other employee in the entire company. Westwood One was a real business with lots of employees working in a very trendy environment. My first impression was very positive.

Norm was very charming, very welcoming and very complimentary. Lynnsey had told him how good my interviewing skills were, and that I was the right person for the position. So Norm was putting on the full-court press. About a half hour into our conversation, I came up with the perfect way to bow out gracefully. I'd make two demands that Norm couldn't possibly meet, but that would leave open the possibility of future employment. I told him that I would only come to work for him if my hours were my own (meaning I could come and go as I pleased), and that I could pull the plug on any interview where I felt I or the company was being abused.

He couldn't possibly let me come and go as I pleased. That would set terrible precedent for all of the other employees who were working traditional eight-hour days. And pulling the plug on an interview meant walking away from possibly the only chance Westwood One would have at getting an artist. I was very proud of myself.

Unfortunately Norm called my bluff; he immediately agreed to my terms. He'd backed me into a corner from which there was no escape. I was embarrassed into accepting the job.

Norm was excited; I was dejected. I had to feign joy. He said that Westwood One's office Christmas party was coming up in a few days, and that would be the perfect opportunity for me to meet everybody. I reluctantly agreed.

****

Rosy Steve Rosenthal

The party was in full swing when I got there. I was stunned. It was being held in the middle of the office, and everybody was openly drinking alcohol. They were all welcoming me aboard, when I suddenly smelled that wonderfully familiar scent of cannabis burning. Within seconds, a joint was passed to me. Now I had two choices. I could turn it down and risk not fitting in, alienating everybody on my first day on the job. Or I could participate and immediately be thought of as one of the gang. I opted for the latter. My initiation was a success.

What I didn't realize was that alcohol and drugs (as well as dirty jokes and sexual innuendos) were not limited to the Christmas party. They were an everyday thing at Westwood One. It was the '80s and the music industry ... and debauchery was part of the job description. We were all in our 20s with 20-somethings' lust for overindulgence. I quickly worked my way up the food chain of depravity and became a leader of the office deviance that would define an entire decade at Westwood One. It was a role that I took very seriously for the next 10 fun-filled years.

Chapter 10

George Harrison: At the feet of living history

March 7, 1979

His single "Blow Away" was released just three weeks before, on Valentine's Day, followed six days later by his eponymous LP. I wasn't sure what to expect. It would possibly be the only time I'd be in the presence of a Beatle. Yes, it would only be a press conference, and I'd be 50 feet away from him. But he was a Beatle and being in the same room as George Harrison would be like being in the presence of living history. The Beatles broke up nearly a decade before, but there was still that Beatles aura.

****

The conference room at Warner Bros. Records is set for about 50 journalists. When I walk through the door, I see that half the seats are taken. I'm never comfortable in a crowd of other journalists. I'm pretty shy, so I'm more than a little out of my comfort zone. But I'd better get comfortable in a hurry. I need to be as close to him as possible in order for my microphone to pick up his voice. Otherwise I'll walk away with nothing.

I look to see where George will set up, but there's no podium … there's no place for him at the front of the room. All of the other journalists are bunched toward the front ... there's no place for me to even get close. When I look around for the best remaining seat, I spy an over-sized chair in the very back. It's got to be ... there's no other place for him. Could every reporter in the room have miscalculated? Am I the only one who's noticed? Or am I the dumbest journalist here?

In part because I can't find a seat up front, and in part because of my intuition, I set up my equipment right at the base of the over-sized chair in the back. If I'm wrong, I'll be too far away for my mic to record him. I'll probably never get another chance, so I better be right. In just a few moments, all of the seats in the room are taken ... all except the over-sized chair. Then the Warner Bros. publicist escorts him into the room, into the only seat available. Right into my sweet spot. I'm sitting on the floor at the feet of the Quiet Beatle ... one of the Fab Four Holy Grails of music interviews.

****

George was anything but quiet that day. He was laughing, joking, down-to-earth and completely at ease. He'd been the focal point of hundreds of press conferences, but he acted like this was fresh, the most important presser he'd ever done. He was the consummate professional in a very sweet and fun way. I got plenty of radio quality material. And more importantly, I walked away with the belief that he was truly genuine.

Me? I'd outsmarted the best and the brightest reporters in Los Angeles. I had the best seat in the house ... right at the feet of living history.

Chapter 11

Sour and Bitter: The Beatles drummers

I'm not sure why, but interviews seem to bring out the worst in Beatles drummers. Where George and Paul had been sweet, that's how sour Ringo was … and (understandably) how bitter Pete Best was.

****

October 27, 1981

It's finally happening. I'm finally getting my chance to interview a Beatle one-on-one. Ringo's new album, *Stop and Smell the Roses*, is being released today, and Boardwalk Records, his new label, has asked me to interview him to help support the LP's debut. There's been much ballyhoo about the release, and I'm flattered that Boardwalk thinks enough of me to be part of such an important day. It's been five years since Ringo's had a successful album, but everyone's hopeful his luck will change starting today.

I arrive early at the posh Beverly Wilshire Hotel in Beverly Hills. I set up my equipment with great anticipation, and within minutes, Ringo enters the room with his wife, ex-James Bond girl Barbara

Bach, at his side. She's as gorgeous in person as she was in *The Spy Who Loved Me*. Let's just say Ringo married up. Being a Beatle certainly has its rewards.

I explain to Ringo who I am and why Boardwalk has asked me to interview him. I let him know that Westwood One will air the interview on hundreds of radio stations around the world in support of the album's release. He couldn't care less. I'm not sure why he's consented to the interview if he's so totally disinterested. Unfortunately, they're both pretty aloof … apparently bored at the thought that they have to spend time with the common man. But I press on. I tell him that we'll talk about *Stop and Smell the Roses* for about 20 minutes, then transition into some Beatles stuff. He understands and agrees.

And we do just that. We talk about the new LP, and things go okay. He's not Mr. Personality, but we'll be able to use what I've gotten so far. It's not earth-shaking, but he's a Beatle, and Westwood One's audience will find it somewhat interesting. Then I transition into historical questions as I do with all of my interviews … background stuff that will keep listeners engaged even if they're not interested in the new material. It all helps sell records … and the artists understand the process and the purpose.

But as soon as I ask the first Beatles question, he begins to whisper (inaudibly) his answer. He knows this is for radio, and he knows he's fucking with me. He knows we'll never be able to use his response. I ask the second Beatles question, and he whispers again. He knew from the beginning that he wouldn't discuss history, so why the hell did he agree to my terms up front. He's being a prick in a passive-aggressive way. After all, he's Ringo Starr. My passive-aggressive way is to end the interview early. He doesn't need the money, and I don't need the aggravation. There are a lot of other artists who appreciate what Westwood One and I can do for them. I'm not wasting any more of my time with an aloof, sour asshole, even if he is a Beatle.

As a sidenote: *Stop and Smell the Roses* stiffed at No. 98 on the *Billboard* album chart. John Lennon would've called it "Instant Karma."

July 12, 1982

Have you ever wondered what it would be like to be inches from stardom? How about mega-stardom? In the annals of history, few have come as close as Pete Best. When Pete's publicist asked me to interview the one-time Beatle, I jumped at the opportunity.

If you're not familiar with Pete Best, he was the Beatles drummer for two years, between August 1960 and August 1962, bookending their now-famous stints in Hamburg, Germany. That's where the Beatles really honed their skills, before returning to England in search of a record deal. If you look closely at photos of the group's early dates at the iconic Cavern Club in Liverpool, you'll see Pete drumming in the background.

Best had quite a following, particularly among the Beatles' female fans, many of whom thought he was the handsomest of the lads. But he was fired from the band just as it was about to become the most famous rock group in history. Different parties tell different stories about why he was sacked. Beatles' producer George Martin acknowledged that he was not enamored with Best's playing and that he wanted a session drummer to play on the group's early recordings. But Martin said it was never his intent to permanently replace Best. Just in the studio sessions.

Martin said he was surprised when Beatles manager Brian Epstein booted Best from the band. Epstein claimed that it was the other Beatles who wanted him dismissed. Paul has been quoted as saying Pete simply wasn't good enough, and George Harrison went on record saying it was he who conspired to get Ringo to replace Best.

Pete Best has become a footnote in musical history … at times a curiosity, other times a sideshow. "Ladies and gentlemen, step right

41

up and see the biggest 'what-could-have-been' in modern times." And I was as curious as anyone to see the curiosity up close.

I was hoping that Pete would be gracious about his tough luck. But he was bitter to the core. He had nothing nice to say about the blokes who he felt threw him under the bus. He said that the others were jealous of his impact on the ladies ... that his drumming was solid and absolutely no cause for dismissal.

Instead, Pete Best became a long-time civil servant, earning civil servant wages. He formed various bands hoping to capitalize on his stint in the world's most famous band. At the time that I interviewed him, he was publicizing two albums, *The Beatle That Time Forgot* and *Rebirth*. None of his efforts have ever garnered him stardom in his own right.

He did gain some notoriety and considerable money in 1995, when the Beatles compilation album *Anthology 1* was released, featuring tracks on which Best played from the group's early Hamburg days.

With a little more luck, he could have been Sir Pete, pushing aside the legendary Sir Paul. Instead, he remains the answer to his own trivia question, "Who is the Beatle that time forgot?"

Chapter 12

It was a night to remember ... but I don't

Monday, June 4, 1979

I'm really pissed ... along with several thousand other fans at the Universal Amphitheatre. It should be a beautiful, fun-filled evening under the stars atop the Hollywood Hills. But Dennis Wilson is smashed, and the other Beach Boys are seething. His drumming is awful, and the band has no way of keeping up with him. It's the most embarrassing display of public drunkenness I've ever seen ... until tomorrow night.

Tuesday, June 5, 1979

The excesses of the music industry have been well documented, but tonight was a night that Atlantic Records out-excessed themselves. Unfortunately, I don't remember too much about the party for the group Bad Company. I out-excessed my previous personal best by about six Jack Daniel's. When you're 26 and living paycheck to paycheck, record company party to record company party, you never know when or where your next JD is coming from. So you feel it's your duty to drink up for all of the unfortunate souls across the globe who can only afford to sip generic bourbon. And so I drank to them all night long.

Bad Company, Jack Daniel's and jumbo shrimp. Does it get any better than this?

It was a night to remember ... but I don't.

Wednesday, June 6, 1979

I wake up with a hangover for the ages. My moustache hurts. Breathing's making my headache worse. Do the ants on the kitchen counter have to be so loud?

I try to piece together what happened last night. I remember something about jumbo shrimp. And Jack Daniel's. Ohhh! Jack Daniel's! My best friend betrayed me.

And I remember humiliation. But why humiliation?

Then I remember! I remember her sitting on my lap. I remember the chair snapping over and the two of us crashing down, right on the dance floor. I remember trying to get up with her on top of me. The harder I try, the more flopping around I do on the slick floor. When we finally make it upright, I can feel the stares. Humiliation. Pure humiliation.

I've got to apologize to her. But I can't remember which her. There were a lot of hers. How do you apologize when you don't know which her you're apologizing to?

But I've got a plan. I start a list of the hers I can remember. Maybe that'll shake the cobwebs.

There was Kathy ... and Linda ... and Elaine ... and Karen ... and ...?

****

One Brain Cell Left

I start at the top. I call Kathy and immediately begin groveling. "I'm sooo sorry about last night." She asks, "What are you talking about?" It wasn't Kathy.

I try Linda. "No, it wasn't me."

Elaine. "It must have been someone else."

Karen answers, and I meekly say, "Hi. It's Rosy." She starts immediately, "I'm sooo sorry, Rosy. I was sooo drunk. I should never have sat on your lap. I'm really sorry. Can you ever forgive me?"

Now I'm in a dilemma. It was my fault. I was way too drunk to be in public. I dropped her in front of all of her record company peers. I had to think fast.

So I say, "You know, I was about to tell you that you embarrassed both of us. That I can never face these people again. But you've apologized, so I forgive you." The old switcheroo. Works every time. Why admit guilt when you can make the other person apologize?

Chapter 13

Fleetwood Mac: My fantasy shattered

Fleetwood Mac in 1977 – (Left to right) Mick Fleetwood, Christine McVie, John McVie, Stevie Nicks and Lindsey Buckingham

Credit: *Billboard Magazine/Wikimedia Commons*

One Brain Cell Left

October 10, 1979

Every once in a while I'd get lucky. One phone call and I'd get an interview lined up. But that was the exception. Most of the time, it took a lot of patience and persistence to book certain more elusive artists. Such was the case with Fleetwood Mac. I tried for a year to get them.

Their *Rumours* LP had won the Grammy Award for Best Album of the Year in 1978. It was No.1 on *Billboard's* album chart for 31 weeks, spawning four Top 10 singles, "Go Your Own Way," "Don't Stop," "Dreams" and "You Make Loving Fun."

Rumours became the fourth-highest-selling album of all time, with more than 19 million copies sold in the United States alone ... more than 40 million worldwide. They simply didn't need my help, but it didn't stop me from trying.

My persistence paid off. More than two and one-half years after the debut of *Rumours*, the group was finally releasing its follow-up, the double LP *Tusk*, on October 12, 1979. I was scheduled to interview Christine McVie and Stevie Nicks two days prior to its release, the same day Fleetwood Mac would be awarded a star on the Hollywood Walk of Fame.

I was thrilled, and not just for scoring the interview. At the time, Stevie was one of the hottest-looking women in all of rock and roll. She was so hot that a punk group, the Rotters, released a controversial single earlier in the year called "Sit on My Face Stevie Nicks." It was a terrible song, but it expressed the desires of millions of young men (and a percentage of young women) around the world. I'd be lying if I said I wasn't one of them.

****

Rosy Steve Rosenthal

Christine is waiting for me. It's 3:00 p.m., our scheduled time, and Stevie isn't here yet, so Christine and I just start to chat in anticipation of Stevie's arrival.

I'm pleasantly surprised. Christine has no inflated sense of self-importance. She's extremely welcoming and easy to talk to. It's often awkward and uncomfortable engaging a celebrity for the first time. But with Christine, it's totally the opposite. She has no overblown ego that's so prevalent in rock stars who believe their own hype.

Ten minutes go by, then 20. Stevie still hasn't arrived, but it's not terribly unusual. In the industry, it's referred to as "Rock and Roll Time." Still, it's apparent that Christine's getting impatient with Stevie ... like this has happened before. Christine and I decide it's best to start the interview. Stevie will join in when she gets here.

The interview flows like an extension of the conversation we were having before the recording began. She's easy-going ... down-to-earth. It's worth the one-year pursuit to finally score such a good interview.

Then Stevie shows up. It's pretty clear that something's wrong. She's having trouble walking, her eyes are half-open, and her speech is slurred. I've interviewed others who were under the influence, but few were this far gone. Christine is livid. She's definitely seen this before from Stevie.

It's always difficult when another artist arrives late, after the interview's begun. The rapport that's been established starts to crumble. The tardy party tries to take over, and the interview begins to disintegrate. That's on a good day. But when the artist is under the influence, things really start to unravel. Today was one of those days.

Stevie feels it's her duty to make up for lost time. But her behavior's so erratic that it's ruining the interview. Christine intervenes when Stevie starts to ramble, but the latter just keeps slurring, overcompensating to try and cover up for her lack of coherence.

Christine can hardly hide her feelings. She's seething. Finally I've had enough of trying to make this work. There's no sense in trying to continue. Stevie's whacked out of her mind. I politely thank them and pull the plug 15 minutes before the interview's scheduled to end.

Poor Christine. The group is about to embark on an 18-month, worldwide tour to support *Tusk*, and she's gonna have to put up with this shit on a daily basis. I'll never get another shot at a Fleetwood Mac interview, but somehow it just doesn't matter to me anymore.

I take particular delight when Stevie gains an enormous amount of weight over the next few years, prompting the Rotters' Phester Swollen to acknowledge, "I've contemplated changing the lyrics to 'Don't Sit on My Face Stevie Nicks.' It's not a pretty thought anymore."

Chapter 14

Never get stoned before, during
or after an interview

October 5, 1982

Today it was two. Some days a bunch of us from Westwood One would drive the 15 minutes from Culver City to Marina del Rey for a margarita lunch. Today I had two. So I was smiling that tequila-Tuesday smile when we pulled back into the Westwood One parking lot. I had just a few minutes to get sober, before I was scheduled to do a phone interview with Carl Carlton. His single, "She's a Bad Mama Jama," was climbing the R&B charts, and he wasn't coming out to LA. So it would be my only chance to grab him, before the song started to fall.

I got back into my office feeling no pain, with just a few minutes to gather myself and head into the studio. Just as I sat down at my desk, my buddy Murray peeked in and told me he had some weed he wanted me to try. Now I'd only been high once during an interview (with a group called Blue Steel) and once immediately after an interview (with Jerry Garcia's former band, New Riders of the Purple Sage). Both were stoned disasters. So I told Murray I couldn't. But he kept badgering me.

One Brain Cell Left

Maybe it was the tequila. Maybe it was the pressure of the moment. Maybe it was just another Westwood One Tuesday afternoon. But to stop the badgering, I took a hit. Then he remembered that the pot wasn't very strong, that I wouldn't even feel one hit. So he told me to take another. Again I protested. Again he insisted. I was running out of time. The interview clock was ticking, so I took another hit. He ducked out of my office, and when he came back just a few seconds later, he grinned a shit-eating grin. The asshole knew he'd had me.

There's that scene in the movie, *Trading Places*, when Eddie Murphy calls out to an incredibly drunk, Santa suit-wearing Dan Aykroyd. Aykroyd glares out through his haggard Santa beard, his eyes dark and swollen, barely open, barely focused, and all he can muster is an ugly, drunken snarl. That was me when Murray returned to my office. I looked up at him, my eyes dark and swollen, barely open, barely focused, and all I could muster was a dreadful, painful snarl. He could hardly contain his delight.

It was in that stupor that I rose up out of my chair and began the impossibly long, 50-foot stagger toward Studio A.

I was a one-year-old learning to walk. I would try to move forward, take a bowlegged footfall to the side and stumble backward two steps. I was swimming upstream against the momentum that kept carrying me backward. And time was running out. The interview was to begin in just a minute.

But I was lucky. The same stumbling momentum that pushed me backward somehow turned into stumbling momentum forward. I crashed precariously through the studio door and willed my way into the seat at the mic, just in time to start the phone interview.

I was in a panic. The tequila-infused pot made thinking unthinkable. Someone had put a dozen cotton balls in my mouth, and I could barely get any words out. There was nothing I could do to prevent the impending train wreck. I was supposed to ask dozens of intelligent, articulate questions over the next hour, but I could barely introduce myself. But Lady Luck must have had some tequila-pot-infused moments of her own.

Rosy Steve Rosenthal

I managed one brief, inane question, and Carl Carlton took it from there. He meandered on and on for 15 minutes without taking a breath. In my inebriated state, I couldn't possibly follow his thoughts, but I didn't have to. He just kept spewing ... long enough for me to compose a second brief, inane question. And he was off again. Another 15-minute answer. A third question ... another 15 minutes. I'd conducted an entire interview, drunk and stoned, with only three questions. I thanked him for the wonderful time we had together.

****

When the interview was over, I looked upward, my eyes dark and swollen, barely open, barely focused. And all I could muster was a dreadful, painful snarl as a thank-you to the interview gods. I slumped back in the chair, basking in my tequila-pot-infused stupor. And I grinned a shit-eating grin.

Chapter 15

John Mellencamp and me: Our dirty little secret

November 13, 1979

I'm not sure what Riva Records was thinking when they asked me to interview an up-and-coming artist named John Cougar at 10:00 a.m. Apparently he wasn't a morning person.

His self-penned "I Need a Lover" was beginning to make some noise in the fall of 1979. Purely coincidentally, I had an interview scheduled a week later with another up-and-comer named Pat Benatar, who'd also recorded the song for her *In the Heat of the Night* LP. So I was aware of the industry buzz around Cougar, not just for his singing, but for his songwriting, as well.

The cover photo of his self-titled *John Cougar* album spoke volumes about the man. He was unshaven, smoking a cigarette and staring deeply into the camera. It was pretty apparent that he was an artist who wasn't going to conform. He was going to make it on his own terms.

****

I show up a few minutes early at the Sunset Marquis hotel in West Hollywood. On a side street just off the Sunset Strip, it's an industry favorite, especially among the non-conforming artists that I've interviewed through the years. Peter Gabriel. Robert Palmer. Adam Ant. AC/DC. Peter Tosh. The stars love it for its seclusion. They can write songs. They can play music into the night. And nobody cares.

The hotel is pretty quiet at 10:00 a.m. I have the operator connect me to Cougar's room.

No answer. I wait five minutes and have the operator try again. Still no answer. I know I'm at the right place. I confirm that I've got the right time. I ask the front desk for Cougar's room number. The staff knows me from all the interviews I've done there. They give me the room number, no questions asked.

I knock on the door. No answer. I knock again. Nothing. I'm about to walk away, when the door flies open, and a disheveled woman says, "Good. I got here early to make sure everything's OK. Bye." She hustles past me down the hall. I realize she's from the record company.

Now I'm pretty naïve, but even I'm not that stupid. I enter the room, and I'm greeted by a half-awake, unkempt John Cougar. The bed looks like it's been rocked all night long. All I can do to downplay this awkward moment is to nod my head and smile. He's not delighted that I'm here. It's pretty obvious he may be a morning person for select things, but being interviewed was not one of them.

"I Need a Lover" barely cracks the Top 30, but it's a start. The album stalls at No. 64.

****

His follow-up LP, *Nothin' Matters and What If It Did*, spawns two Top 30 singles, "This Time" and "Ain't Even Done with the Night." But he still hasn't broken through.

One Brain Cell Left

Then comes "Hurts So Good" under the new name John Cougar Mellencamp. It's the hit he's been waiting for since his first album was released in 1976, when he was known embarrassingly as Johnny Cougar.

April 12, 1982

I know he wouldn't remember me, so I explain that I'd interviewed him a few years ago at the Sunset Marquis. I tell him the story about the record company woman awkwardly greeting me on her harried way out the door. I ask him if he has any idea what happened to her.

"I married her," he sheepishly replies.

My jaw drops. My eyes bug out. "But you told me you were already married!"

He then tells me that he'd been having an affair with Vicky, flying her to his gigs all across the country. He'd fallen in love with her and told his first wife, Priscilla, who granted him a divorce so he could marry Vicky.

The dark, distant John Cougar of 1979 finally lets his guard down. He seems to enjoy our dirty little secret. Smiles don't come easily for him, but this time he manages a guilty one. Even the patently stoical John Cougar Mellencamp has to laugh. He'd been caught with his hand in the cookie jar.

Chapter 16

Free drinks, a blind hockey goalie and a goat

Fall semester 1973

An informal meeting before the college ice hockey season:

Howard: I wanna get Rosy on our team.
Tom: But he's a terrible player.
Howard: Yeah, but he's sports editor of the school newspaper.
Tom: But he's a terrible skater.
Howard: Yeah, but he can get the team a lot of publicity.
Tom (dejectedly): Yeah, I guess you're right.

And that's how my illustrious college hockey career began. I couldn't skate. I couldn't shoot. I couldn't pass. But I controlled whether or not the Cal State Northridge ice hockey team got into the school newspaper. The very definition of power. Intoxicating power.

It turns out I wasn't the only player who power-bribed his way onto the team. A teammate we'll call Dwayne Gretzky had a father who owned a seedy bar not far from campus. It was the kind of bar where you'd bring your own Lysol and paper toilet seat covers ... just for the glasses. When Dwayne was with us, we'd be lavished with free

drinks after the games. We'd drink as only college students can drink
… long into the night. The drinks would flow until we ran out of
Lysol and toilet seat covers. Then we'd go home and shower for
hours trying to wash away the seediness. Somehow you just never felt
clean.

The free drinks gave Dwayne the intoxicating power to pick
whichever position he wanted to play. He chose goalie. I should
mention that Dwayne was clinically blind. He couldn't see more than
a few feet in front of him. His Coke-bottle glasses barely helped. An
opposing player would take a shot from center ice, and Dwayne
wouldn't move. He couldn't see the puck coming, so when the shot
banged against the boards behind him, he'd jump straight up like a
frightened cat. It got so bad we started calling him Mr. Magoo, after
the blind cartoon character. Try skating when you're already a terrible
skater and your own teammates are whistling the Mr. Magoo theme
song.

Dwayne couldn't see. He was a terrible goalie. But you can put up
with a lot when Jack Daniel's and lemon-flavored Lysol are at stake.

A few minutes into the first game of my hockey career I got the
puck about 20 feet from the other team's net. I took an
embarrassingly weak shot that floated sky high. When the puck
reached its apogee, like a dying duck it fell straight downward behind
the goalie, hit him on the butt and somehow caromed into the net.
Unbelievably, I'd scored a goal on my very first shot in college. I was
the hero of my very first game … until the last few seconds.

The score was tied, and there was a furious scramble for the puck
in front of the other team's goal. Their harried goalie had been sent
flat on his face, way out of the net. I ended up in the goal crease with
the puck right underneath me. All I had to do was tap it about six
inches into the empty net for the game-winning goal. The puck lay
there for an eternity, while I thrashed about trying to keep from
falling. When my legs started flailing like a Cossack dancer, the other
team swooped in and knocked the puck clear of the net ending the
game. I was a morbidly desperate Charlie Brown watching Lucy rip

the puck right out from under me. My own school newspaper said I went from hero to goat in the same game.

I wouldn't score another goal until my last game in college. In between I had my nose broken, took a pointed stick to the top of my head making me see stars, tore ligaments in my ankle twice and got a huge knot on my shin from continually blocking shots without shin guards. The knot wouldn't go away for a year and a half after I stopped playing. But it was the most fun I ever had playing sports.

The highlight of my hockey career came when we played UCLA at the Fabulous Forum, the home arena of the NHL's Los Angeles Kings. UCLA's captain was such an asshole that when I put a crushing hit on him, his own teammates cheered. After the game, we showered in the Los Angeles Lakers locker room. It was the biggest thrill I ever had in a shower that didn't include sex with or without another person.

That was it, the only season I ever played in college. When I left the newspaper, the team no longer needed me. As any deposed despot can attest, intoxicating power can be fleeting.

Chapter 17

Escape from the Planet Shame

May 4, 1979

My most impressive display of interviewing artistry came not with a superstar, but with a singer I'd never even heard of.

In the spring of 1979, Chrysalis Records' publicist called to ask if I would interview an artist she said was the former front man for the group Mott the Hoople. Somewhere in the recesses of my mind, I'd heard of the band, but I had no idea what type of music they played. I wasn't even sure if I'd ever heard one of their songs. But I agreed to interview the now-solo Ian Hunter anyway. I often did favors for publicists with the hope that they'd return the good deed and get me interviews with their big stars. Plus, I might get lucky. The artist could later get airplay, and I'd have the interview in the can when I needed it. More often than not, the strategy worked. Chrysalis would later repay me by delivering interviews with such top artists as Pat Benatar, Billy Idol, Huey Lewis and Joan Jett.

Rosy Steve Rosenthal

||*|*|*|*|*|*|*|*|*

The morning of the interview, I look frantically around my apartment and realize the publicist hasn't sent me a copy of Ian's album or bio. This is long before the World Wide Web. I have no way to go online and look up background info on Mott the Hoople or see Ian perform on YouTube. But it's not the worst thing. I can show up early at the record company, listen to the LP there and read up on him. I've done it several times before when a label forgot to pre-deliver the goods.

I show up at Chrysalis an hour early and get lucky. As soon as I arrive, the publicist comes out of her office. I'm about to tell her that I never got the package and ask her for the album and materials, when luck turns to panic. Ian Hunter emerges from behind her. "Great," the press agent says. "The last guy didn't get his package and canceled, so we can start right away."

Now the publicist's a friend of mine, and I don't want to throw her under the bus in front of her client. So I do the right thing. I agree to start early and follow them into the conference room in complete and utter humiliation, knowing I know nothing about this man. My credibility's at stake. I'm sweating bullets. Word could get out that I came to the interview totally unprepared and crashed and burned. The record company publicists all know each other and they talk. I'm screwed.

I set up my equipment and have no choice but to start the recorder. I'm seconds away from shame, when I rhetorically say, "It must be a completely different feeling with your name on the record, not having to hide behind Mott the Hoople."

Ian jumps right in. He responds by talking about the pressure being squarely on his shoulders. He implies that if the album fails, he has no one to blame but himself.

One Brain Cell Left

As he talks, I listen and follow up on what he's just said. His answer leads to my next question ... and the next, and the next. This goes on for 45 minutes. When we end, Ian gushes, "It's great to finally meet somebody who knows something about me!"

Chapter 18

Mickey Mantle swore at me

That's me and Mickey Mantle holding up scorebooks from a 1962 Yankee doubleheader in which The Mick hit three home runs.

One Brain Cell Left

July 18, 1985

By far my biggest idol as a child was Mickey Mantle. No one else was even close. All of the book reports I wrote in junior high school were on various biographies of the Yankee slugger. You could hear my classmates groan every time I'd say, "My report today is about Mickey Mantle." They'd heard it so many times before.

Some 20 years later, in 1985, a former high school classmate-turned book publicist named Nancy called to ask if I would do an interview with Mantle for the book *The Mick*. I was crawling out of my skin with excitement.

Growing up on Long Island, my parents would take my brother, Ira, and me to the old Yankee Stadium for a doubleheader. It was our annual birthday present. We would buy scorebooks and keep a record of every at bat in the two games. I was seven years old and knew every Yankee's batting average and how many home runs he'd hit. I learned division to compute batting averages before I was 10.

So when I got the call to interview The Mick, I immediately phoned my brother. He sent me scorecards from both games of a 1962 doubleheader and asked me to show them to Mantle. Mickey'd hit a total of three homers in the two games ... quite a feat.

The night before the interview, the publicist, Nancy, called and said that she'd been having a lot of trouble with Mantle. He was an alcoholic jerk. That really got to me, but at least I'd been warned.

****

I'm standing in the hotel room with more butterflies than I'd experienced since I walked into Yankee Stadium for the first time as a seven-year-old. I'm in the presence of the man who meant more to me than JFK. I shake his hand and can't believe it's really happening to me.

Never before have I had such a reaction. I've prided myself in the fact that I almost never was in awe of a celebrity. I was 21 when I began my professional journalism career and looked 16. I had to be every bit as professional as the person I would interview, in order for them to take me seriously.

But I never met Mickey Mantle.

I pull out the scorecards and say, "Mick, I don't know if you care, but I've got scorebooks from 1962. You hit three homers in the doubleheader." I place them on the table and proceed to set up my recording equipment.

A minute later, I hear an angry voice boom out, "I thought you said I hit three?!"

"In the doubleheader, Mick." I hear him rifling through the pages, when he realizes what I said.

"Oh."

Mickey Mantle holds in his Hall of Fame hands the scorebooks that we'd saved for more than two decades. It actually means something to him to see how he'd done that far-away day. It means even more to me.

He regales me with stories from the old days, when he was lightning quick and more powerful than any man in baseball. The interview ends all too quickly for me.

I ask if he'd record a promo for the show. He reluctantly agrees. Certainly not a pleasant response, but it'll be over soon. I hold out the sheet of paper from which he'll read. I put it about a foot from his eyes. He moves it arm's length away.

I'm oblivious. I'm only 32 and know nothing about a 53-year-old's deteriorating vision. So I persist in moving the paper closer to him.

One Brain Cell Left

"I told you to get the fucker away from me," he growls. The owner of three MVP awards and seven World Series rings has just sworn at me. My all-time idol.

No junior high school book report could've prepared me for that.

Chapter 19

The Golden Age of Sexual Harassment

A conversation overheard in the Westwood One offices:

Poppy (indignantly): Rosy, all you wanna do is get laid!
Rosy (indignantly): I take offense at that. I wanna get blowed, too!

The record industry. Pre-sexual harassment laws. Pre-Don't Drink and Drive. Pre-AIDS. A recipe for disaster ... and a helluva lot of fun. Westwood One in the early '80s was the traveling Wild West Show ... and I was elected ringmaster. I campaigned on the platform that moderation was to be stricken from the record. We wanted more sexual harassment ... more alcohol ... more drugs ... more sex ... and more rock and roll. It resonated throughout the company. With both men and women. And some barnyard animals, too.

First, let me apologize on behalf of myself ... and all others like me. Today's sexual harassment laws are on the books because of us. Now that I've gotten that out of the way ...

I took my responsibilities seriously. Whenever a new woman came to work at Westwood One, it was my job to find out about her sexual history. I had a brotherly way about me. Even those women who thought their sex life was private would open up to me within 20 minutes. Even when they saw it coming, they were still helpless. In a matter of minutes, they happily professed their love of oral sex … both giving and receiving. They boasted of their one-night-stand track records. Things that were generally not discussed in mixed company in the early '80s. Especially with someone they just met. But it was a time and a place and an industry that brought out the slut in all of us. Librarians need not apply. We all gravitated to the record industry because of the thrill of overindulgence.

One female co-worker at Westwood One was generally a grumpy, unhappy downer. But I always knew when she'd gotten laid the night before. She had a special glow about her, and I busted her every time. She hated that I could tell, but she couldn't keep the smile off her face when I did.

Going out for margarita lunches was the norm. Then we'd go back to the office and get high. We all had pot to share, and no one cared, as long as we got our work done. Coke was readily available, too. One of my co-workers even bragged that he'd put $85,000 up his nose.

It was an atmosphere that can never be duplicated, because of today's laws … and because of political correctness. Believe me, I understand. But it's sure made for a dull workplace. As a corporate consultant after leaving the music industry, I NEVER talk about sex at a client's office. But it's funny. My experience is that women feel that they have a wide-open playing field now that men must behave. They've perfected their dirty-talk skills, while mine have atrophied. I've swung back to being a prude. Now I'm actually embarrassed when a woman says something sexual to me. Like when she proclaims she doesn't just wanna get laid … she wants to get blowed, too.

Chapter 20

Duran Duran: Topless Like the Wolf

July 28, 1982

"Rosy, I really need you to do this interview for me." It's a refrain I'd heard over and over again from desperate publicists. Record company publicists have a difficult job. The media are only interested in artists when they're hot. When it's a newer artist, especially one whose last record stiffed, the PR people come begging.

Steve Gelber from Capitol Records caught me at the wrong time. I'd just come back from Nashville, where I'd done 10 interviews in three days. I spent my Fourth of July on an airplane flying back to LAX. I had eight interviews scheduled the following four-day work week, and another 14 the week after that. That's 32 interviews in 18 days. I was in no mood to do another favor for a publicist.

Gelber wanted me to interview a British group whose last record couldn't even make *Billboard's* Hot 100 chart. I knew of Duran Duran from their single "Girls on Film," which was only played on a handful of New Wave radio stations. That was it. The song died a horrible death. So when Gelber called, I just wasn't interested.

Then he pulled out all stops. "But Rosy, we're softball buddies. You gotta do this for me."

The year before, I'd formed the first Westwood One softball team to play in the entertainment league. I'd played competitive softball for 10 years. It was my passion. Sometimes I'd play in three leagues at a time. So in the spring of 1982, when the commissioners of the entertainment league decided to let the league dissolve, I stepped up and anointed myself commissioner. Steve Gelber was

68

captain of the Capitol Records team. He knew how to play my guilt. He knew I couldn't turn my back on a softball blood-brother. I caved.

****

Gelber sends me the shortest bio I've ever seen. Capitol Records can't even fill one page with Duran Duran background information. And now I'm supposed to do an hour interview with a group I couldn't less about interviewing, armed with nothing. These are the times when I miss working the fry vat at McDonald's.

****

I haven't been to the Chateau Marmont since John Belushi OD'd there four months ago. It's an iconic castle hotel nestled in the Hollywood foothills overlooking Sunset Boulevard. Opened in 1929, it was named a Los Angeles Historic-Cultural Monument in 1976. It's been home to countless entertainment industry personalities ever since. On this day, it's home to a little-known British rock and roll band.

I call from the lobby, and their manager summons me to the room. I walk passed the pool and see something I've never seen before in LA. Several beautiful young women were basking topless in the hot July sun. I assume correctly that they're guests of the little-known British rock and roll band. It's my first inkling that these boys may be bigger than I thought. I think about asking the young women if they need someone to apply sun tan lotion. But I have work to do. They'll be applying SPF to me in my fertile imagination when I'm alone tonight.

****

About five minutes into the interview, I'm already running out of questions to ask, when one of the boys mentions that they shot a video in the jungles of Sri Lanka. I'm not even sure where Sri Lanka is, but it sounds pretty exotic, so I decide to follow that path. They tell me the video's for a song called "Hungry Like the Wolf." They say it evokes images of Indiana Jones, with rivers and elephants and marketplaces. They share their trials and tribulations of shooting in a steamy jungle. They relay that guitarist Andy Taylor was hospitalized from a stomach virus he'd caught when he swallowed lagoon water during taping. Interesting stuff, but I'll probably never be able to use it, unless their careers suddenly take a u-turn for the better. I leave hoping to get one last look at the young women's beautiful ... personalities.

****

"Hungry Like the Wolf" isn't released for another four months. More than six months after my interview, the song finally finds its way into *Billboard's* Top 10. Westwood One is sitting pretty with the interview already in the can. I call Steve Gelber to arrange another interview. "Steve, I really need to talk to the band again. Remember, we're softball buddies. You gotta do this for me." Needless to say, my begging didn't help. I never interviewed Duran Duran again. And more disappointedly, I never saw their topless aficionadas ever again. But somehow I still remember what they look like. Both of them.

Chapter 21

I was a teenage bookie

October 4, 1967

While most 14-year-olds were earning spending cash babysitting, I began my reign as a ninth-grade bookie. I booked bets on the World Series, Super Bowl, horse racing ... any sport my classmates chose. I loved the thrill of doing something illicit ... and the money was pretty good, too.

I ran back-to-school gambling specials in September so I would gain notoriety come the big score ... the World Series in October. Guys I didn't know would seek me out to place bets. I developed quite a reputation as I moved into high school, and a nice little following, too. So much so, that the boys vice principal cornered me in the bathroom one day and said, "I know what you're doing. You'll be in big trouble when I catch you." I was flattered. I had no idea he knew who I was. I'd arrived as a bookie.

The crowning jewel of my bookmaking career came on Sunday, January 12, 1969. Super Bowl III. The underdog New York Jets of the American Football League versus the 18 ½-point favorite Baltimore Colts of the NFL. The huge point spread worked in my favor. I was able to set it up so that I couldn't lose. I'd win money whichever team won the game. I'd really arrived as a bookie.

71

I was a huge Joe Namath fan at a time when few gave the Jets any chance of winning the Super Bowl. New York's 16-7 upset was the catalyst for the two leagues finally merging, something unthinkable just months before. And me? I smiled all the way to the piggy bank. My favorite player on my favorite team just won me some spending cash.

None of my classmates ever welched on a bet. How could they? I had a 400-pound enforcer who would collect the money. Who's gonna say, "Screw you. I ain't paying," when they knew Big Dave would be stopping by to collect?

I'd become pretty infamous as a bookie. There was one time when we had to do a report in health class. The teacher told us we could pick any subject we wanted for the report. "Rosenthal, you're doing yours on Gamblers Anonymous." I was the only one he'd singled out. My reputation preceded me wherever I went in school.

So I went to the North Hollywood Library to do some research. I found a 14-question survey that Gamblers Anonymous used to determine if you had a gambling problem. If you answered four of the 14 with a Yes, you had a problem. I answered 10 of the questions with a Yes. But I wasn't deterred. I was shooting for a perfect score.

The more money I made as a bookie, the more emboldened I became. I got careless. I thought I could never lose. Then one day a classmate booked a horse racing bet on a 30-to-1 shot named Huxley. I knew almost nothing about horse racing, but my bravado told me I would never lose.

Huxley lost by a nose that day. If he'd won, I'd still be paying for it.

The odds were stacking up against me. I was taking bad bets ... taking too many risks. The boy's VP was out to get me. My teachers were on to me. Gamblers Anonymous told horror stories about gamblers losing everything. My girlfriend threatened it was gambling or her.

And besides, Big Dave had graduated. I had no one but myself to collect the money. And I was 132 pounds soaking wet. I was a teenage bookie whose reign was over. It was time to hang it up. My Hall of Fame bookmaking career was finished at the age of 17.

Chapter 22

Did Joe Namath have a man-crush on me?

March 25, 1987

It was the only time I'd totally lost my professional cool as an interviewer ... the only time I'd stop the tape in the middle to gush as a fan.

Alongside Mickey Mantle, Joe Namath was my sports hero. He oozed cool. Fur coats. Pantyhose commercials. He loved the spotlight, and the spotlight loved him. He was the perfect idol for New York sports fans. And although I'd moved to LA from NY before the Jets drafted him, I followed his career as closely as any New Yorker. I remain a New York sports fan. Even to this day.

Broadway Joe became the face of the old American Football League. He was brash, outspoken and fun-loving. You never knew what outrageous thing he would do or say next. But above all, he was a Hall of Fame quarterback.

Los Angeles had no AFL team in 1967, but I was able to follow the Jets on TV. Their games were frequently broadcast nationwide to take advantage of Namath's star quality. I knew every player on New York's roster. I knew no one else in my high school that cared anything about the AFL. LA only cared about the NFL's Los Angeles

One Brain Cell Left

Rams and their stars Roman Gabriel and Merlin Olsen. Little *House on the Prairie's* Merlin Olsen.

So when the Jets won the Super Bowl in 1969, I had classmates congratulate me, as if I had something to do with it. For me, Namath became larger than life.

****

I get a phone call from a high school friend of mine, Dean Bender, who's started his own PR firm. He wants me to interview Joe Namath to promote a new TV show that Namath is hosting. Would I be interested?

My heart begins to race. Me, the one who prides himself in being aloof ... the one who never gets flustered about any interviewee. I stammer, "I'll be happy to." I'm hoping that Dean doesn't catch on to the quiver in my voice.

Namath greets me at the front door of his Beverly Hills home. He's gracious and welcoming, nothing like I expected. There's none of the brashness that he exuded during his playing career. I do the best I can to hide my man-crush.

The interview is going well, but I'm having trouble concentrating. As we talk, my stomach is screaming with butterflies. I've never experienced any feelings this strongly before, and I can't take it anymore. About 25 minutes into the interview, I do the unthinkable. I stop the recording and gush, "I've done more than 1000 interviews, but I've got to tell you, Joe, this one really means something to me." He's heard this tens of thousands of times. He graciously thanks me. Nothing more. I restart the tape, thoroughly embarrassed that I let my professionalism go by the wayside.

When the interview ends, we chit-chat about his playing career. I begin to break down the equipment. Then I say, "I know you won't remember this, but there was this meaningless play that for some reason stands out to me. You hand the ball off to Abner Haynes. He sweeps left, sees 11 defensive jerseys about to crush him, so he turns around and laterals the ball back to the first Jet he sees. It's you, and you get creamed, right in front of Weeb." Weeb Ewbank was the Jets' cartoon character-like coach, who wore a crewcut in the days of long hair.

Namath had terrible knees and needed constant protection. It was a grotesque mistake to give him the ball in the open field without five or six players blocking for him. "On TV, you could all but see Weeb's crewcut turn beet red," I tell him.

Namath can hardly contain himself.

He excitedly calls out to his wife in another room. "Deb, you've got to come in here! You've got to meet Steve! He's the real deal!" It's his way of acknowledging I'm a superfan, different than the hordes of casual fans he's met through the years. The ones who know him from the Super Bowl and pantyhose commercials and little else.

It was one meaningless play that meant absolutely nothing in the scheme of things. 1967. Abner Haynes played a total of three games for the Jets in his entire career. He carried the ball just 16 times, and Joe and I remember that one obscure play.

And just for that one fleeting instant, the tables turned. Could it be? Did Joe Namath just have a man-crush on me?

Chapter 23

Westwood One's Christmas parties would be illegal today

Suddenly, there was loud pounding on the studio door. "Rosy, I know you're in there!"

"Go away!" I yelled back.

"Rosy, open the door!" "Get outta here!" I commanded ... to no avail.

Murray wouldn't give up. He kept barking at me to open the door. I finally had no choice. He was gonna keep pounding until I did. So I opened Studio B's door ... half-naked ... with a half-naked woman I'd just met lying on the floor. It'd been a great Westwood One office Christmas party so far. But Murray was ruining it.

He thought I had the cocaine. I didn't. I was having sex. I didn't care who had the cocaine.

I glared at him. He saw I was indisposed. He looked down and saw a half-naked stranger on the floor of Westwood One's brand new, never-before-used recording studio. He turned 17 shades of red and politely excused himself. I closed the door and went back to what made this year's office Christmas party especially great. A wonderful Friday night at Westwood One.

On Monday, I sauntered into the office around 10:00 a.m. Everyone was already working. I hadn't even sat down yet, when Norm Pattiz, Westwood One's owner, yelled at me across the office, loud enough for everyone to hear, "What the hell were you doing in my brand-new studio?" Murray had ratted me out. Now everybody in the office knew. I turned 17 shades of red. Then I looked at Norm. He was smiling a Cheshire-Cat smile. He wasn't mad at all. In fact, he nodded his approval. He actually seemed proud of me. It was, after all, a Westwood One office Christmas party. Another great one for the history books.

Sadly, the one day a year that I really looked forward to would be illegal today. Because of people like me.

Chapter 24

Tina Turner, Phil Collins and the pain of divorce

Credit: Philip Spittle

April 10, 1979

She's at the lowest point of her adult life, still reeling from her bitter divorce from ex-husband, Ike Turner. She's broke with no record contract. Her last two albums didn't even chart. She's surprised that I want to talk to her.

It's a bit unusual for me. I rarely interview celebrities who aren't hot at the moment, least of all one without a record deal. But Tina Turner's timeless. As a young teenager, I remember her being the closest thing to rock and roll porn. She was absolute raw, unabashed eroticism, singing and dancing like nothing I'd ever seen before … undulating pure sexual energy on stage. And that voice. Pure, gruff soul that crossed from rhythm and blues to rock and back in the same song. I was excited to meet the first woman's inner thighs that I'd ever seen.

I track her down through her new manager, Roger Davies. We decide to do the interview at Davies' Santa Monica office across the highway from the Pacific Ocean.

The interview goes extremely well. Tina and I just click right away. After we stop recording, we decide to continue the conversation. Then she really opens up, about the physical, mental and emotional pain of her divorce and how she still hasn't recovered a year after it was final. We talk as if we've known each other for years. We talk about how my marriage is struggling and how difficult it would be to leave my childhood sweetheart.

She pours her heart out to me, and it's heart wrenching. But it's also cathartic for her … just to get things out. The change in her is dramatic in just the few hours that we spend together.

And it leaves a lasting impression on both of us.

One Brain Cell Left

December 20, 1982

It's an emotional time for me. My wife and I have just split up for good after 12 years together. She was my high school sweetheart ... the first girl I ever dated. And even though I'm the one who wants the divorce, I'm still getting over losing my best friend.

It's been more than two years since Phil Collins divorced his first wife, Andrea Bertorelli, but he's still recovering. He, too, is in an emotional state.

His 1981 LP *Face Value* spawns the hit single "In the Air Tonight." The album cuts a somber look at his failed marriage.

Now he's released a new album, Hello, *I Must Be Going!* featuring a cover of the Supremes' smash "You Can't Hurry Love." It's this latest project that brings us together, but it's our divorces that form our bond.

I'm not used to talking openly with another man about personal things. Women and emotions are familiar and comfortable to me. Talking with another man is not. But for some reason, Phil and I find comfort in sharing our divorce experiences.

I feel for him. Here's a man who seemingly has everything ... fronting the top-selling group, Genesis, and riding the success of his Top 10 solo album debut. But he still can't get over his wife leaving him for another man. He's dating a woman, American Jill Tavelman, who will become his second wife. But he's still battling demons from the end of his first marriage.

My story pales in comparison to his pain. I leave the interview with the new reality that things could be a lot worse. At least my divorce isn't being played out in the tabloids.

Rosy Steve Rosenthal

May 9, 1984

Five years after I met Tina Turner, she lands a new contract, signing with Capitol Records. The label sends me an advance copy of the album *Private Dancer*, and it's absolutely fantastic. I call Capitol, and we set up an interview for May 9, 1984, three weeks before the LP's release. I wanna make sure I get the interview in the can before the record explodes. I know if I wait too long, she'll be in demand all over the world, and my window will be gone. I'm that confident *Private Dancer* will be a monster success.

I'm waiting in Capitol's publicity department when she emerges with a half-empty bottle of wine in her hand. She's giddy from the alcohol, but it's obvious that it's more than that. She's basking in the newfound respect with which Capitol treats her. I hardly recognize her from five years ago. She can't get the smile off her face.

Then she sees me. The alcohol makes her especially excited. She gushes, "I remember you! I even remember what we talked about! We talked about my divorce!" She remembers me being there for her, when her life and her career were at a painful standstill.

It's one of those rare moments that transcends the excesses and superficiality of the record industry. After all that she's been through, it's great seeing her so happy. It's a wonderful feeling knowing she cared that I was there for her when she needed it most. And it's given me hope that there's life after divorce.

Chapter 25

Kareem Abdul-Jabbar:
The tallest asshole I've ever met

December 11, 1981

The pop you're about to hear is the sound of my bubble being burst.

****

Lew Alcindor was my favorite college basketball player of all time. He led UCLA to three straight NCAA championships in the late '60s. He signed with the Milwaukee Bucks as the first player selected in the 1969 NBA draft. In his second season, he led the NBA in scoring, won the MVP award and guided Milwaukee to the league championship. Right after the Bucks won it all, Lew Alcindor, who'd converted to Islam while in college, adopted the name Kareem Abdul-Jabbar.

****

In September 1974, I began my professional journalism career as producer of a radio sports talk show at KGIL in Los Angeles. I chose what guests I wanted on the show and tried to find a way to get them in studio. One long shot was Kareem Abdul-Jabbar. He was fairly self-conscious and reticent about doing interviews, but I had an idea how to get him.

I knew Sam Gilbert had an office in the San Fernando Valley, not terribly far from the KGIL studios. Sam was a UCLA super-booster who'd taken under his wing the shy Alcindor/Abdul-Jabbar and other Bruin players, earning Gilbert the nickname Papa G. I gambled that Papa G was familiar with our show and gambled that he still had sway over Kareem. I was 21, extremely ballsy and feared calling no one. I got Sam on the line on the first try.

Gilbert took an immediate liking to me, in part because, like him, I was Jewish. I think he saw a lot of him in me, especially the ballsy part.

And my ballsiness worked. The long shot paid off. He got me Kareem.

****

Sam Gilbert was first through KGIL's back door. He was affable and delighted in playing the Godfather. The second through the door was the tallest skyscraper I'd ever seen. Sam introduced me to a quiet and shy Kareem Abdul-Jabbar. He was nice in a timid kind of way. I led him to the booth where he'd field questions from the radio call-in audience.

Kareem answered the callers' questions in a patient, quiet way … always pleasant, but very quiet. It wouldn't have made for interesting radio if his name wasn't Kareem Abdul-Jabbar. He seemed thankful when it was over.

****

One Brain Cell Left

In 1981, Westwood One started producing a sports program called *The Competitors*. Among other things, athletes would talk about their interests outside professional sports. I knew Kareem practiced martial arts, a perfect tie-in for *The Competitors*.

He'd been traded from Milwaukee to the Los Angeles Lakers six years earlier. LA's home arena, the Fabulous Forum, was only minutes from the Westwood One studios. I called the Lakers and told them I wanted to interview Kareem regarding martial arts. They approached him with my request, and he agreed to meet me in the locker room after the team's practice.

****

When I arrived at the Forum, everything had been pre-arranged. I was led to the Laker locker room, the same locker room where I'd showered seven years before as a player on the Cal State Northridge ice hockey team. Laker players, staff and a lot of media were hanging around. When Kareem entered, I approached him, introduced myself and told him I was the one who was there to interview him regarding martial arts. He was prepared for me.

Once I turned the recorder on to start the interview, for absolutely no reason, he began to demean me, putting me down in front of everyone in the locker room ... nothing whatsoever to do with the interview. It was completely out of left field. I was in such a state of shock that I can't even remember the things he was saying ... just the shitty way he was saying it. Maybe he didn't like my long hair. Maybe it was a hazing ritual. I have no idea. But he wanted to show everyone in the locker room that he was a big shot. They were all laughing, which motivated him to disgrace me even further. I'd done nothing, said nothing that would've provoked such an out-of-the-blue, mean-spirited attack. For him it was a game to be played in front of a live, approving audience.

I was blindsided. He was no longer the pleasant, quiet person I'd met at KGIL years before. He was loud, obnoxious and utterly shameful.

Finally I'd had enough. I shut down the recorder before the interview was supposed to end, completely humiliated. I left the locker room with my tail between my legs. I've never been treated like shit that way by anyone else in my life.

My bubble was burst. My favorite college basketball player of all time turned out to be the tallest asshole I've ever met.

Chapter 26

Always wear a cup when you play tennis

Spring semester 1972

When I was a teenager, I excelled at most sports. My tennis serve was an absolute rocket. It struck fear in the hearts of many a player … mostly on the next court over. It was like golf. As soon as I hit the ball, I'd yell out "FORE!" You'd see players scramble from fear on adjacent courts as my "absolute rocket" whizzed by their ears. I was terrible. I knew I needed help. So in my freshman year of college I decided to take a tennis class to fulfill my P.E. requirement. I figured it couldn't hurt. I was wrong.

As the semester dragged on, my play got worse and worse. In fact, there was only one player in the class worse than me. We'll call him Sean McEnroe. One day Sean and I faced each other knowing the loser would be shamed forever. No one remembers the second-to-worst. They only remember the worst.

I'd watched Sean play enough times to realize he didn't even need the strings on his tennis racket. All of his shots ricocheted softly off the wood on the outside of the racket. His volleys would then fly weakly in a high arc just over the net, where his opponents would smash each return into smithereens. Sean had no chance. I would employ the same strategy … rush to the net and wait for each of his dying ducks to fall from the sky. Then I'd smash the return beyond Sean's feeble reach. It was my recipe for success. I'd show him who the worst in the class was.

My plan worked perfectly. I'd wait anxiously at the net for each of his wood-aided volleys to fall from on high, then I'd just kill the return. Shot after shot gave him absolutely no hope. With each pop-up, my feet danced like a four-year-old needing desperately to pee. My whole body would tremble uncontrollably in anticipation of my next smash. I was destroying poor Sean. The more devastated he looked, the more frenzied my feet, the more hysterical my swing. I smelled blood. The inevitable victory was within my frenetic reach. I could retire knowing I wasn't the worst. Victory, sweet victory would be mine.

Then it happened. I would forever remember my disgrace. One last dying duck. One last out-of-control dance. One last out-of-control swing. I swung so violently that I missed the ball completely. The full force of my wild, vicious follow-through arced through the air in front of me and caught me squarely in the nuts with my own racket. I was writhing in mid-air, even before my tumbling body bounced off the unforgiving pavement. My agony was only exacerbated by my utter humiliation. The pain was so great that I couldn't even open my eyes, but I could hear the joyous laughter of my classmates, male and female, as they encircled my convulsing body. I thrashed around like a freshly caught marlin on the deck of a trawler.

I was told that I didn't open my eyes for 18 excruciating minutes. When my world finally came into focus, I realized that I'd unknowingly crawled from one court to the next. It took another few minutes before I discovered that I'd only smashed my left one. Then how was it possible that everything screamed with pain from my nipples to my knees?

One Brain Cell Left

Sean McEnroe won on a forfeit that beautiful spring day. With birds merrily chirping and butterflies fluttering by, I lay agonizingly, despondently on the court knowing that I would live forever with the humiliation that I was worst-in-class. I walked gingerly, bowleggedly off the court with my tail between my legs. Okay. So it wasn't exactly my tail.

Chapter 27

Did I really call Lionel Richie an asshole to his face?

November 19, 1982

My sense of humor could best be described as really sick. I was sick long before Eddie Murphy and Sam Kinison. In fact, when people would say, "Rosy, you're sick!" I would take it as a compliment … I'd succeeded at shocking them. I made fun of myself first and foremost, and that gave me license to poke fun at everything and everybody. Nothing was beyond my boundaries. Gays and straights, blacks and whites, the mentally and physically challenged. I found the humor in everything. I'd poke fun of bigots by saying outrageously racist things … statements that no one could possibly take seriously. Well, maybe bigots thought I was serious. My sick humor was always for its shock value. And I was my No. 1 target. People would say, "Your sense of humor is so self-deprecating." And I'd respond, "That's because I have so much material to work with."

When I first started doing interviews, an African-American friend of mine from college, George Wanamaker, was head of publicity for Black Music Marketing at CBS Records. George had been my Third World Editor when I was Co-Editor-in-Chief of the newspaper at Cal State Northridge. He and I would exchange outrageously racist statements pointed at each other, and we both knew that it was all in good fun.

One Brain Cell Left

One of George's BMM publicists, Gene Shelton, wasn't quite sure. He heard these outrageous things coming from my mouth, and he was shocked. Gene was very prim and proper. He dressed immaculately in an industry where every day was Casual Friday. George had to convince Gene that I wasn't a racist. It took a while for Gene to realize that I didn't mean anything I said. Gene and I eventually became good friends, but he was always shocked at the things I would say.

Gene was such an excellent publicist that he was hired as head of PR at Motown Records. In the fall of 1982 he called me to do an interview with Lionel Richie. Lionel had just released his self-titled debut album, and the first single, "Truly," was on its way to becoming No.1 on the *Billboard* pop chart. He'd been the front man for the Commodores, who had five Top 10 albums, and now he was on his way to an even more successful career as a solo artist.

We decided to do the interview at Lionel's home in Beverly Hills. When I arrived, Lionel was upstairs, so Gene and I had some time alone. This was a big day for Gene. He wanted to make a good impression with Motown, but he knew I was a loose cannon, and he begged me to be on my best behavior. I loved Gene, but you never give an arsonist a match.

A few minutes later, Lionel made his appearance. To shock Gene, my first words to Lionel were, "So they tell me you've become a real asshole since you gained all this success." Gene is a dark-skinned African-American, but I swear he turned white. His absolute worst fears were realized. Even after Lionel and I both started laughing, Gene looked like he was going to pass out.

It was the perfect icebreaker for Lionel and me. The interview went really well, but something seemed off. He wasn't smiling. He wasn't as happy as you'd expect with the success of his debut record. After the interview ended, we had a long, off-the-record conversation. I soon realized why he was down.

Lionel and his Commodores bandmates had been together for 14 years. They'd gone to college together. They grew up together, endured the tough times together and realized their success together. Now Lionel felt guilty that he was experiencing success on his own.

I said to him, "Two things. One: You're not doing this TO the band ... you're doing this for yourself. Two: the Commodores were a success before you became the face of the group. You're not giving them credit that they'll be successful without you."

You could see his face change; he realized I was right. At least for the moment his guilt went away, and he could enjoy his solo stardom. It made me feel good to see him smile.

****

On the drive home, I realized the significance of what I had said to Lionel. I'd been unhappy in my marriage, but I felt too much guilt to leave my wife. Now it occurred to me. One: I wouldn't be leaving to hurt her. I would be doing it for myself. Two: She was a complete person before I met her. I wasn't giving her enough credit that she would have a good life without me.

That night I told her I would be leaving. It was a conversation with Lionel Richie that gave me the courage to move on with my life.

Chapter 28

A machine gun and explosives

December 21, 1979

I woke up with the flu, and I felt awful. My first wife, Diane, had left for a doctor's appointment, and our 15-month-old son, Landon, was asleep in his crib in the other bedroom. I went back to sleep hoping that I'd feel better when I got up.

Later that morning, Diane returned home, came into the bedroom and tried to rouse me, but I wasn't interested. I just wanted to sleep. Finally, she threw a scrolled up piece of paper in my direction and told me to read it. Again I wasn't interested, but she was persistent. I unfurled the paper, and it read, "Pregnancy test positive." At first I was groggy and it didn't sink in. But suddenly I realized what it meant, and I became ecstatic. I had always wanted four kids, and now I'd be halfway there. My flu suddenly didn't feel so bad.

My elation didn't last long. There was a loud banging at the front door. It wasn't unusual for friends to knock loudly. From our bedroom, you couldn't hear a normal knock, so people had to bang on the front door to get our attention. Diane went to see who was there. I threw on a pair of pants to greet them.

As I reached the living room, there was a loud commotion, and several men pushed through the door passed Diane. They rushed me and one hurriedly pressed a gun into my forehead. I had no idea what was going on. As someone who'd never been in any trouble before, I was scared shitless.

One of the men was wearing a police uniform. It seemed almost surrealistic. The one with the gun in my forehead proclaimed, "You know why we're here?" I answered quizzically, "No?" He repeated, "You know why we're here?" Again I replied, "No?"

There were now about six frenetic "peace officers" in the living room. From the back, I heard one shout, "Did you read him his rights?" Another shoved some papers in my direction. It was a search warrant. I began to read, but it made no sense to me. I said, "I'm pretty intelligent, but I read very slowly. If you tell me what you're here for, maybe I can help."

"A machine gun!"

I let out an audible laugh, which made them even angrier. I'd never held a firearm in my life, let alone a machine gun. They made me sit down and began to search the entire apartment. I read the search warrant. It wasn't just for a machine gun. It was for all sorts of explosives, too. My paranoia was intense. All I could think of was that they were going to take me away from Landon and my unborn baby for something I had nothing to do with. I was in a panic ... a clinical panic.

Every second felt like an eternity. They left about an hour later without so much as an apology. No explanation of why they thought I'd have such lethal weapons. Every cabinet door, every drawer was open and the contents molested. I felt completely violated, like I was living in the Soviet Union.

I reread the search warrant. Suddenly I realized there were two addresses listed: ours and another that belonged to a friend who lived about a mile away.

Eleven days earlier, shortly after 5:00 p.m., I received a call from the same friend. He wanted me to help get him an attorney. I asked why? He said that social services were at his house, and they were taking away his kids. I told him the only lawyer I knew was a corporate attorney. He asked if I could try anyway. I told him it was after 5:00 and that the attorney's office was closed, but I'd come over if he wanted me to lend some moral support. He said he'd really appreciate it.

I arrived at his house a few minutes later. Several cops were there, but his kids were already gone. I sat quietly with him for some time. As I got up to leave, one of the cops handed me a slip of paper and asked if I could write down my name and address, just for the record. My entire criminal record consisted of one speeding ticket going through Utah three years earlier, so I willingly wrote down my information and left. I had no reason to believe that would turn my life completely upside down.

I had no idea my friend was involved with weapons, let alone such violent ones. So when the cops pushed their way into my apartment, I was completely dumbfounded. Because I'd offered moral support, the cops "knew" I was involved. They'd obviously obtained an illegal search warrant, but they didn't care. As long as they "got their man," it was okay to lie to a judge. It would be feathers in their caps toward promotions. They couldn't care less that they had turned me into a clinical paranoid manic depressive for something I had nothing to do with.

Later that night, on the 11 o'clock news, the lead story was about the cops finding explosives at my friend's home in North Hollywood. The cops drove in a long caravan through bumper-to-bumper Friday night rush hour traffic to an open field about 15 minutes away. There they detonated the explosives on live TV. Had a reporter found the simultaneous search warrant at my friend's home, I have no doubt that I would've been part of the ensuing media circus.

Several days after the cops came to my door, I was awakened around five in the morning by another loud knocking at my front door. It was the asshole cop who'd had his gun pressed into my forehead. "Remember me?" he asked sarcastically. I smirked,

"Unfortunately!" I was no longer afraid. I had nothing to lose by being sarcastic. He'd already broken me.

He handed me a subpoena to appear in court. No apology. Just a subpoena. I asked him why they'd illegally targeted me. He said someone had told him I had a machine gun. I told him that was bullshit … that anyone who knew me knew I'd never even held a real gun. He just smiled … a smile that said, "Fuck you. I'm a cop, and I can fuck you over anytime I want."

The subpoena only intensified my paranoia. Every time an ambulance or fire truck drove by my apartment with sirens blaring, I knew they were coming to take me away. Every time I looked in my rearview mirror and saw a police car, I knew they were tailing me. My clinical paranoia and manic depression lasted nearly six months. I was a completely shattered human being. Somehow Diane remained calm and in control throughout the whole ordeal. She knew I had nothing to hide.

For a year, they would come to my door with subpoena after subpoena. I would go to court, they would never call me to testify, and the cycle would start all over again. Because I had written my name on an innocuous slip of paper, I was now part of the court record.

The only person I could think of who might know why the cops had come to my door was my friend's nine-year-old daughter. When I asked her, she confessed that, after being grilled for hours by the cops, they asked her if she knew "Steve Rosenthal, who has a machine gun." Of course she knew me. She told me she didn't know how to answer the question, so she said, "Yes." And that was how they obtained the search warrant. By twisting a nine-year-old into answering a question that was despicably misleading. They had absolutely no evidence that I was involved, so they made it up. I certainly never blamed the girl. She felt terribly and apologized profusely to me. But the subpoenas just kept coming. Finally, after a year of me protesting that I had nothing to offer in the case, they removed me from the subpoena list.

One Brain Cell Left

****

Diane gave birth to a beautiful, red-haired baby girl eight months later … our daughter, Torrey. If the cops had their way, I would never have seen her or Landon ever again. The contemptibly illegal actions of the cops caused me to lose to severe mental illness what should have been a very happy six months of my life.

Fuck you, LAPD. Fuck you for being so shameful. Fuck you for never even apologizing. And fuck you for making me never, ever trust another cop as long as I live.

Chapter 29

Steve Wozniak and his pissed-off wife

November 16, 1982

She was really pissed off. "Why are you calling him at home?" she demanded. Actually, I didn't blame her. It's bad enough to have to share with the world your famous husband when he's at work. But a phone call at home is a true invasion of privacy. "How'd you get this number?" she asked angrily.

Candice Clark was a star in her own right. She was an Olympian and a national and world champion in canoeing and kayaking. More than most, she understood the media attention that came with success. She also knew when a journalist overstepped his bounds. But I had an excuse.

****

Candice Clark's husband was Apple Computer co-founder Steve Wozniak. Unlike most programmers, Woz loved the fame he attracted. In fact, he sought it out. Mind you, this was decades before he'd seek notoriety by dating Kathy Griffin or competing on *Dancing with the Stars*. No. His lust for the spotlight had been there from the beginning.

By 1982, he'd made so much money through Apple that he'd underwritten a pet project … the three-day, star-studded US Festival. A musical lineup meant to rival Woodstock. The Police. Pat Benatar. Tom Petty & the Heartbreakers. Jackson Browne. Fleetwood Mac. Santana. The Grateful Dead. Twenty acts that were all major headliners in their own rights.

Westwood One had secured the US Festival radio broadcast rights. And that's where I came in. I needed an interview with Wozniak to round out Westwood One's shows. I called Apple to try and track him down. I figured I'd get a long line of gatekeepers who'd give me the brush-off, but I had to start somewhere. I explained to the Apple receptionist why I wanted to talk with Woz. She happily said, "Let me get you his home number." It was that simple. I asked, "Are you sure it's okay to call him at home?" "Not a problem," she replied. Obviously, she hadn't consulted Candice Clark.

****

"Apple gave me the number," I sheepishly told Clark. "Oh," was all she could muster. She begrudgingly handed the phone to her husband. Unlike his wife, Woz seemed genuinely pleased that I called. I told him that we needed an interview for our radio shows. He was more than happy to oblige.

"When will you be down here in Southern California?" I asked. "When do you want me?" he responded. "Well, when will you be here next?" "When do you want me?" he repeated. He said he would fly down in his private jet to meet me whenever I wanted, then he'd fly right back home to the Bay Area. I told him it could wait until he was down in LA on other business. He'd have none of it. We settled on November 16th. I could just see Candice seething. Not only was I invading their privacy at home, but he now cheerily offered to fly down to LA solely to meet with me. It couldn't be easy being married to a guy who'd ultimately lose some $9 million to $12 million dollars on an impulse just so he could add "Concert Promoter" to his resume'. Now he's wasting money on a private jet just to do one lousy interview with a guy she was already pissed off at. She couldn't have been happy.

****

He, of course, showed up at the Westwood One studios in a limo. He loved playing the celebrity. This was Woz flying in as a rock star who'd gained the notoriety of a world-class concert promoter. He'd rubbed shoulders with Sting and Petty and Benatar. He basked in the attention. And when we were done, he got back in the limo and immediately flew back home. He reveled in knowing he'd just played the big shot pop icon. And I delighted in the fact that this icon thought I was big shot enough to fly down and back just to do an interview with me. I'm sure he got an earful from Candice.

Notoriety has its price. They were divorced five years later.

Chapter 30

My musical roots

Sinatra. Sammy Davis Jr. Tony Bennett.

There was a lot of music in my house growing up in the late '50s in Plainview, Long Island, New York. But almost no rock and roll. My parents were 32 and 31 when Bill Haley rocked around the clock. Another year older when Elvis hit. But rock wasn't my folks' thing. They had their own generation of music. Jazz. Big Band. Blues. Standards. It set the stage for my lifelong eclectic musical tastes.

We had little money, so it was a surprise when my parents splurged on a new, state-of-the-art hi-fi system. I played their records all the time with the sweet sounds pouring off the then-pristine turntable. Sinatra's "Come Dance with Me!" … Tony Bennett's "I Left My Heart in San Francisco" … Sammy Davis Jr.'s "What Kind of Fool Am I." Beautiful standards. But one song in particular changed me forever. In 1959, they bought a copy of Ray Charles' "What'd I Say." I was a six-year-old, little Jewish white boy. I had no idea what the lyrics meant, but I knew I couldn't sit still in my chair. That tempo, that voice, that soul, that grit … the keyboards, the horns, the back and forth with the Raelettes. I mean, I really couldn't sit still. It was my bridge to rock and roll. It was also the root of my love of R&B, which would define much of my career as a music journalist. I was fortunate to later interview many of the artists that shaped my affinity for R&B. The Temptations. The Four Tops.

Smokey Robinson. Wilson Pickett. Tina Turner. Gladys Knight. So, so many. But it all started with Ray Charles.

My uncle Izzy had a special impact on my fledgling love of rock and roll and R&B. He owned juke boxes in bars and restaurants throughout New York City, and when a record had run its course and was being swapped out for a more current hit, Izzy would give my brother, Ira, and me his used 45s. I had a sizeable collection before I was eight years old. Ricky Nelson. Del Shannon. Dion. The Marvelettes. I played them over and over again until the record needle would wear out. Then I'd play them some more, trying to eke out every last drop, as I strained to make out the music through the crackle and mud of the worn needle. New needles were an extravagance, like the old baseballs we'd envelop with electrical tape when the covers tore off. Money was always tight as we struggled through post-war, middle-class suburbia. We made due with the kind of ingenuity poor Brooklynites brought with them to find a new life in the band-box developments of 1950s Long Island.

In addition to "What'd I Say," one other record stood out above the rest ... "The Twist" by Chubby Checker. His *Your Twist Party* was the first album I ever bought with my own money. I did the "Mexican Hat Twist" (named for one of Chubby's songs) in elementary school. I won a twist contest at sleepaway camp when I was nine. And today it's still the only song that can get me off my ass at weddings. I have, embarrassingly, absolutely no rhythm, but you don't need rhythm to twist. Besides, by the time "The Twist" is played at weddings, I've had just enough alcohol to lose my inhibitions. I twist up a storm until my lungs and legs give way, then I sit back down huffing in a pool of sweat, satisfied that I'd fulfilled my quota of one dance per wedding with Marla. She's a great dancer. It's a shame she's saddled with a klutz like me. But she goes in knowing that I'm good only for that one vigorous twist. I guess she's happy to take what she can get.

One Brain Cell Left

As a side note, 20 years after I bought *Your Twist Party*, I would interview Chubby. He was just a nice, unassuming, approachable guy. It meant a lot to me to meet one of my first two musical idols. I'm just sorry I never met Ray Charles. That would've come full circle for me. Unfortunately, some things are never meant to be. Today, more than a half century later, I still can't sit still when I hear "What'd I Say." Some things are meant to be forever.

Chapter 31

I've been a same-sex marriage supporter since 1975

Spring 1975

It was an uncertain time for gays and lesbians in America. Many states still had anti-sodomy laws on the books aimed specifically at homosexuals.

I was a 22-year-old senior completing my journalism degree at Cal State Northridge. I was also employed at my first professional job in radio, as a newswriter and producer at KGIL in Los Angeles

The call-in news show that I was producing was entitled "Comment and Commentary," with host Jim Martin. We were the odd couple. Jim was in his mid-40s and extremely conservative, one of the only conservatives I knew. I was an extreme social liberal, the same age as his son. But we had great mutual respect, and he gave me complete latitude to pick the program's topics and guests each night.

In the mid-1970s, the vast majority of gays and lesbians were still in the closet, unwilling to risk the intense discrimination perpetuated by much of the straight world. The rise of Gay Liberation spawned even more vitriolic responses from those threatened by the call for civil rights. I decided our show needed a spokesperson from the gay community to rebut the bigots. But there was a problem ... I'd never met a single gay who was publicly out of the closet.

Cal State Northridge had a Gay Student Union, one of whose goals was to support its members against rampant prejudice. I decided to attend a meeting to see if GSU could help me find a guest for our program, one who could withstand the impending assault from Jim Martin's patently conservative audience.

****

The GSU meeting had already started when I walked through the back door. All heads turned toward me, and it was apparent by the abundant smiles that many were more than happy to welcome me. I awkwardly announced, "It's not what you think. I'm not here to join the club." I detailed the reason for my visit, and the leader offered the name of a gay reverend, Bob Sirico, who had become a leading advocate for gay rights in LA.

The next day I contacted Bob. He said he would be pleased to be a guest on the show and asked if he could bring along an Australian national ... a man who had married his American partner with an official Boulder, Colorado marriage license. But this was 1975. The feds wouldn't recognize their marriage and were trying to deport the Australian, Tony Sullivan.

Sullivan's husband, American Richard Adams, had petitioned the Immigration and Naturalization Service for Tony's permanent residency, routine for married heterosexual couples in similar situations. The official INS written response, on behalf of the entire United States government, was terse. "You have failed to establish that a bona fide marital relationship can exist between two faggots."

****

Bob Sirico and Tony Sullivan arrived early at the KGIL studios, and the three of us talked for some time. Tony was devastated by the government's denial of residency. It was evident how much he loved Richard, and it was truly heartbreaking to hear their story. It was a defining moment in my life. How could the government deny basic civil rights to any two consenting adults who chose to marry?

I've been an outspoken supporter of same-sex marriage in the four decades since.

****

The call-in show didn't go well for the two. Two-and-a-half hours into the three-hour program, there hadn't been one supportive caller. Only attacks. Then a woman called in and said she'd been listening to the whole program and was so disappointed at the way Bob and Tony had been treated. She supported Tony and Richard's right to marry, but, she joked, "Every time I see a good-looking man who turns out to be gay, I think, 'What a waste!'" The Reverend Bob Sirico replied, "That's funny. Every time I see a good-looking man who turns out to be straight, I say, 'What a waste!'"

****

In 2009, I found Bob Sirico online and emailed him to let him know how that one meeting had changed my life forever. I wrote, "I felt compelled to thank you and Tony for demonstrating how your activism has impacted the lives of those that you couldn't possibly know ... (That) one seemingly innocuous chance meeting has meant a lifetime of my proud support" for LGBTQ.

Bob Sirico's response was a shock. "How mysterious the turns our lives take. ... Within a few years of being on that program, my life too took a somewhat dramatic turn, first politically and a little later, spiritually, in my return to the Roman Catholic Church of my youth." He continued, "For whatever part I may have played in engendering in you a sense of empathy in your approach to others, I thank God. (There is too little empathy in our world today). For whatever seeds of political or moral confusion I may have sown back (then), I repent. (There is too much political and moral confusion as well, some of which I contributed to mightily 34 years ago)."

Bob Sirico had completely changed his beliefs on homosexuality and same-sex marriage. He was now repenting for ever supporting the Gay Liberation movement … repenting for opening my eyes to the injustices imposed on LGBTQ. He wrote that he hadn't had any contact with Tony or Richard in nearly 25 years.

****

It took 40 years after Richard and Tony's 1975 wedding for the United States Supreme Court to rule in favor of same-sex marriage. Tragically, Richard Adams died in 2012, never having seen his marriage to Tony Sullivan recognized by the United States government … the unrelenting government that officially singled them out as "faggots" 37 years earlier.

Chapter 32

Mr. Sakamoto is still holding on line 5

I was a master practical joker in my prime. I pulled phone pranks on publicists at virtually every record company in LA in the days before Caller ID. I'd disguise my voice and pretend I was a writer from a lowly newspaper in Keokuk wanting an interview with one of their biggest stars. I'd do it just to hear the publicists squirm to find a polite way to deny the interview request. Then I'd fess up just to hear them yell at me. "Rosy, you bastard!" "Rosy, you son-of-a-bitch!"

It was all in good fun, and once the publicists got over their initial anger, they actually thought it was funny. It was a tool I used to get the record companies to remember me, and it was pretty useful when it was time for my genuine interview requests.

When you called the record label, unless you knew the person's direct dial, your call went through a live receptionist, who would invariably route you through to publicity, when there was nowhere else to turn. Publicity was the dumping ground for all the whackos that called in, and the department was already crazed with legitimate work. They handled all of the publicity requests when the label's artists were brought to LA or were elsewhere on tour. They put together the packages for reporters, handled reasonable ticket requests and made cold calls to journalists to see if the latter were interested in interviewing the company's artists.

One Brain Cell Left

To be honest, publicists were pretty easy pickin's for a halfway decent prankster like me.

Thus the stage was set for my favorite prank of all-time on a publicist friend, Josephine, from Atlantic Records. In those days, Atlantic had about 50 phone lines, all of which displayed on one huge phone base in every office. You'd see all the buttons lit up like a Christmas tree when the lines were in use.

So one day, I call Josephine, and in a high-pitched Japanese accent, say, "Thees a Tatseo Sakamoto from Tokyo News Agency. Would rike to do interview with Mr. Rou Glamm of gloup Foreigner." The accent isn't great, but it's convincing enough under the pressure of the moment. Josephine gets daily requests for interviews with Foreigner's Lou Gramm, so it seems legit.

Josephine doesn't know what to do with this one. She's obviously swamped, and although it sounds like a legitimate request, she's never heard of the Tokyo News Agency, because it doesn't exist. She has no interest in talking to a journalist she's never heard of and is too stunned to blow him off. She's gonna need a moment before she can come up with an excuse to turn him down. She stammers, "Uhh ... Uhh ... Could you please hold, Mr. Sakamoto?"

It takes a couple of minutes for her to return to the line. "Hi Mr. Sakamoto." I interrupt and say, "Josephine, this is Rosy. What are you talking about?" She says, "Uhh ... Uhh ... Rosy, hold on a minute."

Now I can all but see her looking at 50 flashing phone lines trying to figure out which one was Sakamoto. Finally, she gives up and comes back to the line and says, "Hi Rosy." And I interrupt and say, "Thees a Tatseo Sakamoto from Tokyo News Agency." Now Josephine is frantic and absolutely perplexed. "Uhh ... Uhh ... Could you please hold, Mr. Sakamoto?"

Again she's searching 50 flashing phone lines to find me. She gives up, punches the button and says, "Mr. Sakamoto." I interrupt again and say, "Josephine, this is Rosy. What the hell are you doing?"

A few more go-arounds and I finally fess up. "Rosy, you asshole!" she yelled. But even she had to laugh. She'd been had by the master. And Mr. Sakamoto, he's still holding on line 5.

Chapter 33

I failed Luther Vandross as a friend

Luther Vandross and Diana Ross

Credit: ImagePros

October 22, 1981

Open foot … insert mouth.

We've all done it. Usually we say something dumb and right away we know we blew it. But it took me two years before I found out I'd repeatedly said something unintentionally stupid, and by then it had cost me my friendship with Luther Vandross.

I first met Luther when we did a phone interview on September 23, 1981, the first of four times I'd interview him. His debut *Never Too Much* LP was released just weeks before, and it was on its way to becoming the first of his seven straight No. 1 R&B albums.

It's usually difficult to develop a great rapport with an artist when you're on opposite ends of a phone line. You can't see each other's eyes or facial expressions or body language. Don't get me wrong, you can still do an effective interview on the phone, but it's rarely as good as one that's in person. That wasn't a problem for Luther and me. We hit it off right away. The more we talked, the more we connected. So much so that we decided we'd get together a month later when he was coming to LA from New York.

On October 22, 1981, we met face-to-face at Le Parc Hotel in West Hollywood. We picked up the interview where we'd left off on the phone. By the time the interview was over, we were really enjoying each other's company. We talked for quite some time afterward and decided we'd get together for lunch the following day. I let him pick the restaurant. He chose Orlando and Orsini on Pico Boulevard, an entertainment industry favorite on the fringe of Beverly Hills.

I found him to be sensitive and vulnerable, not as happy as I'd expected him to be with the budding success of his first solo album. Being overweight was a big issue for him. He was very self-conscious. But there was something else. I couldn't put my finger on it.

One Brain Cell Left

Whenever we'd get together, it was more of the same. We got along great, but he still wasn't enjoying his life as much as you might expect. He said he was sad that he wasn't in a relationship. I told him I thought he should be happier ... that women swooned over him ... that he'd have his pick in due time. But it didn't seem to matter. I later found out why.

Although he never acknowledged it in public, I discovered that Luther was gay, and like many gay recording artists at the time, he remained closeted for fear that coming out would spell disaster for his career.

And I never picked up on the signs. In fact, the more I talked about his hold over women, the more insensitive it became. Later, when I found out that he was gay, I felt so humiliated, I stopped reaching out to him. I certainly didn't care that he was gay. I just couldn't face him knowing how uncomfortable I must have made him feel. When it came time to interview him again, I sent one of my reporters rather than face him. To this day, it's one of the things that I regret most about my radio and records career. I took the cowardly way out rather than apologize. My insensitivity ended our friendship.

A few years later, I took Marla to an industry party at Genghis Cohen, a trendy Hollywood Chinese restaurant that catered to an entertainment industry clientele. Luther was there, sitting alone at a booth near the door. Our eyes met, and we awkwardly acknowledged each other. To break the ice, I took Marla over to meet him. He was friendly in a reserved way. It was clumsy at best. That was the last time I ever saw him.

Luther's life was marked by historic successes and terrible tragedies. In 1986, he was speeding in Laurel Canyon when he lost control of his car, and in the ensuing crash, one of his passengers was killed. His public eventually forgave Luther, and his career rebounded with Grammys and superstar collaborations. But in 2003, he suffered a major stroke from which he never fully recovered. He died two years later. He was only 54 years old.

I never got to apologize to him. I always intended to, but the Genghis Cohen party wasn't the place or time to do it. Besides, it's hard to get the right words out when you've had your size-10 Nikes halfway down your throat. As a friend, I choked. Luther deserved better.

Chapter 34

Even Hugh Hefner didn't have the balls to do it

March 21, 1974

We had to make a very tough decision. As Co-Editors-in-Chief of the Cal State Northridge school newspaper, Kim Kent and I were in a major bind. It was the most newsworthy event on campus in years, but if we ran the photos, we'd be facing serious consequences.

****

The streaking craze had spread like wildfire across college campuses in 1974. Now it had streaked through CSUN. Well, maybe not streaked. It kinda romped its way through.

On the morning of March 21, 1974, our *Daily Sundial* campus newspaper was tipped off that streakers were planning a "spontaneous" sprint through the campus at noon that day. So we were ready. We sent photographers to snap exclusive shots ... but they were far from alone. Rumors had already spread throughout the university, and thousands of anxious students lined the tops of buildings and across the quad, awaiting the spectacle. As Kim and I wrote in the next day's *Sundial*, "A man and a woman wearing nothing more than sneakers, socks and infectious grins jogged merrily across campus amidst wild cheers from the largest crowd to assemble at this institution since the Teledyne demonstrations of May 1971." So it wasn't exactly spontaneous. And it wasn't exactly a political demonstration. And it wasn't exactly a streak. But it was a spectacle.

The huge crowd emboldened the couple to the point where they slowed down even further to splash nuditarily through the sprinklers. Then they ducked cheerfully into one of the buildings, taking with them their sneakers, socks and infectious grins … and their 15 minutes of fame. Within minutes, two other couples joined in on the naked fun. Unfortunately for the male streakers, it was cold that day, and there was a great deal of shrinkage.

****

Today, student sexting is relatively common. But in 1974, nude photos were taboo. And that was the dilemma. We couldn't just ignore such a big campus news event. We could take the safe route and airbrush the photos, but Kim and I decided that was the chickenshit way out. Years later, on the 40th anniversary of the CSUN's founding, the *Los Angeles Times* would recount, "Unlike the mainstream media, which showed streakers from somewhat modest angles, the *Daily Sundial* illustrated its story with front-page photographs of full frontal nudity." Not even *Playboy* ran full frontal nudity on its cover. Another 10 years later, in its official 50th anniversary publication, Cal State Northridge named the cover the school's de facto No. 1 campus news story of 1974.

****

Normally, few students bothered to read the *Sundial*, but when I arrived at school the next day, I couldn't find a single copy in the campus newsstands. Sex sells, especially when it's free. The front page caused a sensation, not just on campus, but in the community as well.

One Brain Cell Left

Poor Zena Beth Guenin, the newspaper's faculty advisor. She had to deal with the backlash. Kim and I knew we could get kicked off the paper, but a few members of the community wanted blood. They forced a hearing to determine if we should be kicked out of school entirely.

****

The Board of Publications, which conducted the proceedings, included School of Journalism faculty, university representatives and community members, one of whom was extremely hostile toward Kim and me during the hearing. He was vehement that we be fired on the spot. We were sweating bullets. Zena was magnificent in defending us, but would that be enough? The Board of Publications asked Kim and me to leave the room as it decided our fate. We waited for what seemed like an eternity, as if we were being held in the principal's office until our parents came to pick us up. I have no idea what went on behind closed doors, but as the Board summoned us back, I was panicking how I was going to tell my parents that I'd been kicked out of school. I knew they'd absolutely freak.

Fortunately, I never had to face that reality. The Board begrudgingly decided in our favor. We were allowed to remain as editors for the last few weeks of the semester. But I'm certain had this been October instead of late in the school year, I'd have been blackballed for life, forever working the counter at McDonald's. "Would you like fries with that, ma'am?" "How about two apple pies for a dollar?"

Freedom of the press had won out, and my parents never knew how close their progeny had come to having to register as a sex offender.

****

Twenty-five years later, I happened to drop in at the *Sundial* offices. I introduced myself to the only person there. She turned out to be Cynthia Rawitch, the paper's then faculty advisor. I told her I was co-editor back in '74, and that the highlight of our year was the streaking issue. Cynthia got wide-eyed and excited, as if I were a celebrity. She eagerly related that the cover was still featured every semester in discussions on freedom of the press in CSUN's Journalism Law class.

I was shocked. That long-ago decision to run full frontal nudity on the cover turned out to be my lasting legacy at my alma mater, even if no one remembers my name. My 15 minutes have lasted four decades. Hugh Hefner would be jealous. Even he didn't have the balls to do it.

Chapter 35

Naked, drunk and stupid:
The legend of the dead caballcro

Spring 1974

Suctioned off in a bizarre car wash incident. That's what happened to the vinyl top on my 1969 Oldsmobile Cutlass Supreme. Yes, I got the insurance money, but I didn't use it to get the top replaced. I wasted it on Jack Daniel's and pizza, burgers and beer.

The car was an utter embarrassment, driving around LA with rusted metal where the vinyl top used to be. None of us wanted to be seen cruising in it, so Fred volunteered. He had a cool Camaro that was his pride and joy. A helluva lot nicer than my Olds. Our friend Sidney called shotgun. I squeezed into the back seat behind Fred.

Our destination was an iconic LA Mexican restaurant … El Cholo … on Western between Pico and Olympic. It'd been there since the '20s … its renown almost mythical in the Los Angeles area. Forty-five thousand Mexican restaurants along the way, but we had to drive 27 miles from Cal State Northridge in the suburbs over the hill to El Cholo in our quest for Mexican food perfection. Little did we know they were known for their margaritas, as well.

College kids. A cool Camaro. Seemingly endless margaritas. The combination from which legends are born. The kind of margarita-infused legends only Mexican caballeros could tell around the open fire.

****

There would be a wait for a table, so we went straight to the bar. They said they would call us when our table was ready, so we figured we'd split a pitcher of margaritas while we killed time. There was no rush. We knew it was gonna be a late night.

Twenty minutes later they still hadn't called us, so we ordered a second pitcher.

Another 20 minutes … another pitcher.

By the time they called us for dinner, we'd killed off a pitcher apiece. When the waiter came to take our order, I saw three of him. I took my chances and ordered from the one in the middle. The three of him nodded their approval.

I took one bite of my food, but was too queasy to eat any more. Twenty-seven miles and a two-hour wait to taste legendary Mexican food at a mythical Mexican restaurant, and I could barely eat a bite. I got a to-go package to take the whole thing home with me.

****

I'm not sure why or how we got there, but late that night, we ended up outside the track stadium on the UCLA campus, far from El Cholo or Cal State Northridge. I couldn't remember much of anything. And, of course, I was feeling no pain. Simply put, I couldn't feel.

One Brain Cell Left

I can't remember who came up with the idea to go streaking, but it was a unanimous decision. We didn't hesitate. In our drunken stupor, we climbed a chain-link fence to get into the stadium and immediately disrobed. At least we had the presence of mind to climb the fence first, before we got undressed. Can you imagine? The paramedics would still be talking about the legend of the three nuts that got hung up on that fence. Six actually.

I'm not sure if you can technically call it streaking, if there's no one around to see you. My adrenaline was surging as Fred, Sidney and I did a naked lap around the empty stadium, knowing I was one security guard away from having to explain myself to the law ... and to my parents. At 21 years old, I'd run away from home before I'd face that humiliation.

When we got back to where we'd left our clothes, I looked down and saw that my right palm was bleeding all the way across. Obviously I'd slashed it climbing the fence, but was too numb to notice. It wasn't easy getting dressed again, with the alcohol and the blood ... and the blood-alcohol. And to pour salt in the open wound, we looked up and saw that a gate had been open all along, no more than 20 feet away. We'd risked our collective boy parts for nothing. We never needed to climb the fence in the first place.

****

A week later, Fred came screaming into my office on campus, inventing eight-letter, four-letter words ... all directed at me. He was livid. It seems in my drunken state on streakers' night out, I'd forgotten something. It took a week of rotting stench for Fred to figure out that I'd left my El Cholo to-go package underneath the front seat of his cherished Camaro ... in the brutal San Fernando Valley sun. It seems my '69 Olds with the vinyl top ripped off was no longer that embarrassing. At least it didn't smell like a dead caballero. I vowed never to take another drink ... until a few hours later ... until a new legend could be born.

Chapter 36

Was he a traitor or an American hero?

August 1, 1977

Traitor. Suicide. U-2.

Eisenhower. Khrushchev. The Cold War.

They were words and names that played out every day on television sets across the globe during the early 1960s. But this wasn't an Ian Fleming spy novel. It was a gripping, real-life story … a notorious embarrassment for the United States government and its citizens.

He was the most famous American spy pilot of the 20th Century, the backdrop for the 2015 movie, *Bridge of Spies*, starring Tom Hanks. Francis Gary Powers became the centerpiece of an international crisis when his U-2 spy plane was shot down over Russia in 1960. His was a household name in the early '60s, a man who, because he chose not to commit suicide, was unfairly deemed by many to be a traitor to his country. His capture led to the Soviet Union canceling a historic superpower summit between Dwight Eisenhower and Nikita Khrushchev at the height of the Cold War.

One Brain Cell Left

Powers was swapped for Russian spy Rudolph Abel in 1962, but his return to America was not universally well-received. Many believed he should have committed suicide rather than allow himself to be captured alive.

Though he was known by most as Gary Powers during the U-2 incident, he was later known by his full name, Francis Gary Powers, Frank to his friends at radio station KGIL in Los Angeles. I worked with Frank at KGIL in 1974-75. I was producing talk shows; he was flying traffic watch.

I had the distinction of turning down Frank's multiple invitations to fly alone with him, as he covered the hellish LA traffic. "Hell no!" I joked with him. "You were shot down! No way am I flying with you!" The truth was, I was deathly afraid to fly in small planes.

I don't know what he was like before he was shot down, but when I knew him, he was an introvert, almost bereft of personality. He never seemed to overcome the stigma perpetuated by an unwelcoming society.

I went on to work at other radio stations after KGIL; Frank moved on to fly a traffic helicopter for an LA television station.

In 1977, I began producing my own radio shows and syndicating them nationwide. One of my programs was called the *Nostalgia News Network*, a look back at historic news events. One of my first calls was to Francis Gary Powers. Frank wasn't interested in being interviewed, but I was persistent. I pulled the "but we worked together" trump card, and he finally relented, albeit very reluctantly. He had stopped doing interviews, and only because we'd worked together did he grant my request. I met him at the hangar in Burbank where his helicopter was based.

During the interview, he described dramatically his thoughts and his emotions as he realized the U-2 had been hit, his fears as he parachuted into hostile Russian territory. Then we addressed the elephant in the room … why didn't he commit suicide? His demeanor changed. He became uncomfortable. He told me suicide was only an option, not mandatory. He was to take his own life only if he felt he couldn't withstand Russian torture. He tried to dispel the rumors, but he knew he couldn't change still-prevalent public opinion that saw him as a traitor.

I distributed the interview nationwide to my affiliates, and it was scheduled to air on August 2, 1977.

On August 1, 1977, I was calling on ad agencies in New York City to try and obtain sponsorship for the *Nostalgia News Network*. I returned to my room at 5:00 p.m. and immediately turned on the radio to catch the news. The lead story described how Francis Gary Powers had been killed that day, when his television helicopter crashed returning to Burbank from covering brush fires in Santa Barbara County.

I was stunned. It seemed almost surrealistic. I had just seen him, just spoken with him. My interview with him was scheduled to air the next day. And now he was gone. Just 48 years old.

On a professional level, my interview was now especially timely ... the last interview he ever granted. But something strange happened. Many of the stations pulled the program scheduled for the next day, believing it was inappropriate to air the show after his death. Others ran the interview, explaining that it was recorded just prior to his being killed.

The cause of the helicopter crash was suspicious. Official reports said that Frank ran out of fuel, but many doubted that such an aviation veteran could allow that to happen. Others said that Frank was simply too inexperienced flying helicopters ... that he was a fixed-wing pilot. Powers' son, Francis Gary Powers, Jr., believes his father misread a fuel gauge that had recently been repaired.

It took far too many years, but in 2000, on the 40th anniversary of his being shot down, Francis Gary Powers was honored posthumously with the Prisoner of War Medal, Distinguished Flying Cross and National Defense Service Medal. It was final vindication for a man, who for four decades had been so unjustifiably labeled a traitor to his country.

Chapter 37

Girl ... I wanna throw you against the wall and FUCK you!

March 8, 1979

They were words no woman had ever said to me, let alone a man.

"Keith, I'm really flattered," I confessed. "But I'm straight. It's just not gonna happen." I really was flattered, and I have to admit, it felt pretty good knowing I had such a sexual hold over another human being. I'd unwittingly become what we called in junior high a "P.T." ... a prick teaser. I'd never given a man blue balls before. At least knowingly.

Keith didn't miss a beat. "Girl, you've gotta let yourself go!" He'd said the same thing to me when we first met at a Barry White listening party a few months before. An African American, he decreed, "I want you to be my White Meat!" It was killing him that he couldn't break my will, at least up to that point.

Keith Barrow was a singer-songwriter and self-proclaimed "Disco Queen." He'd gained a fair amount of notoriety in discos, as much for his flamboyance as for his music. For shock value, he told me, he once showed up at a New York club wearing nothing but a leather G-string.

He'd had some success the year before with an R&B/dance tune called "You Know You Wanna Be Loved." Here, he's saying the same thing to me. But I wasn't going for it. "Friends," I told him. "Just friends."

****

The listening party was scheduled at the legendary and exclusive Chasen's restaurant, adjacent to Beverly Hills. It was common for record companies to host their parties at LA landmark eateries, knowing that journalists couldn't refuse a free meal. I was no exception.

Barry White's upcoming LP, *I Love to Sing the Songs I Sing*, would be released within a month. Gene Shelton, the CBS Records publicist, asked if I would interview Barry at Chasen's before the party. I was happy to. Another CBS artist, Keith Barrow, would also be there, and we agreed that I'd interview Keith right after my interview with Barry.

****

Chasen's was a throwback, harkening to its premiere in 1936. It was a heralded Hollywood meeting place where iconic movie deals were developed, and Oscar-party invites were only for the elite. It was an understatement to say the restaurant regulars formed a Who's Who of the entertainment world. They were the most famous and recognizable faces on the planet. Sinatra, Marilyn Monroe, Cary Grant, Clark Gable ...

****

One Brain Cell Left

I'm in awe of the place. Me? I can barely scrape up a tip for the valet. I'm way out of my comfort zone. I'm better suited for Chili's than Chasen's. I walk in, and I suddenly feel better. I see a lot of familiar faces ... all the journalists who came for a free meal and couldn't afford to tip the valet, either.

Gene Shelton comes over to say hi. He's found a nice, quiet place for the interviews and leads me to it. I sit in a booth where I imagine Marilyn's famous derriere once made an impression.

Barry White walks into the room and I'm immediately struck by the man's size ... he's a mountain. Contrast that with the fact he's incredibly refined, and you've got a man of amazing presence. Then he speaks. A simple hello and my balls feel like they're going to explode. His voice is so deep, I can feel my chest rattle.

Barry never lets his guard down. He plays the Barry White character to the max. He's intimidating, yet friendly, and he's a great radio interview. When we're done, he exits, readying to play royalty at his own elegant listening party.

****

Enter Keith Barrow ... the complete antithesis of Barry White. Slender and as effeminate as any man I've ever met.

He's incredibly charismatic. Warm, fun, funny. Totally engaging. We hit it off immediately. By the time the interview ends, we're best friends. We continue the conversation long after we stop recording.

Keith tells me his mother's in the inner circle of the civil rights movement with the Reverend Jesse Jackson. The conversation grows all the more interesting from there ... so interesting that we lose all track of time. Then we hear Barry White's new album booming from the next room. I excuse myself and head towards the music.

I open the door and 100 sets of eyes turn toward me, with Keith glowing immediately behind. It's a major faux pas on my part. You

127

just don't show up late to a Barry White listening party, especially at Chasen's. I turn and say goodbye to Keith and embarrassingly begin searching for an empty seat at one of the banquet tables. I spy the only two seats available, way in the back, and I slink toward them, with Keith in tow. He's well-known in the room, and I assume everyone thinks we're a couple. As it turns out, that's just what he wants.

We continue our conversation over lunch. When the listening party ends, Keith tells me he'd like to see more of me. I explain to him that I'm the horniest heterosexual he'll ever meet, but if he can accept that, I'd love to see him again. Without missing a beat, Keith squeals, "Girl, you've gotta let yourself go!" I stand firm on my orientation. We schedule a date to see each other again, when he comes back from New York. It turns out, he's bicoastal.

****

When he returns to LA, he calls me to get together. I drop everything and go see him. I meet him at his apartment, we go to lunch and really enjoy each other's company. But he wants more.

When we get back to his apartment, he proclaims, "Girl … I wanna throw you against the wall and FUCK you!"

****

I'd told my wife about my special friendship with Keith. She wasn't sure what to make of it. Then one day, when I was out doing interviews, Keith called and my wife answered. "Girl … I'm gonna steal him away from you!" he pronounced in his most queenish voice. At least, that's the way Keith re-enacted it for me later.

When I got home, my wife couldn't look me in the eye. She hemmed and hawed and finally, sheepishly, asked, "Steven, are … are you gay?" It was an opening too good to be true. I jokingly replied, "I guess technically you can't call it gay ..." And I walked away smilingly. I thought it was funny. She was crushed. She couldn't tell if I was kidding or not.

****

Keith would call every month or so and we'd meet up. We had a lot of fun together and shared serious times together, too. But he never stopped trying to convince me to "let myself go." Then in November 1979, I walked away from the entertainment industry, just about the same time Keith's calls stopped. A year later, when I resurfaced at Westwood One, I tried to reach him, but his phone number was disconnected. I was disappointed, but I knew we'd reconnect down the line.

Several years later, I was at lunch with two CBS Records publicists, when I asked if they knew how to reach Keith. Their faces dropped. And my worst fears were confirmed.

Keith Barrow died of AIDS-related complications on October 22, 1983. He was only 29 years old, the youngest of all my interviewees to die. He'd apparently contracted HIV during the time that we'd been seeing each other in 1979 ... two years before the CDCP even recognized AIDS. There but for the grace of God and a Quaalude go I.

Chapter 38

Mel Brooks
and one of the great blunders of my life

April 1, 1982

Did I do something to upset him? Did I say something to offend him?

Why was Mel Brooks chasing after me … running down the stairs, yelling after me to wait?

****

1968. I was 15 years old. On the TV, Steve Allen was interviewing a small man, a director I'd never heard of. The diminutive guest was talking about his upcoming movie titled *The Producers*. They began showing a clip, a musical number from the film. I was immediately appalled. "Springtime for Hitler" was in terrible taste, a song and dance number singing the praise of the most hated man of the 20th Century.

It took a minute before I got the joke. When I did, I began laughing uncontrollably. "Springtime for Hitler" was a hysterical spoof of the Nazi people and their despicable leader … at a time when the horror of the Holocaust still festered in open wounds the world over. Mel Brooks had tackled head-on the most sensitive of subjects … and nailed it. Humor eclipsed hatred. I became a fan for life. *Blazing Saddles. Young Frankenstein. High Anxiety. History of the World Part I.* A true comical genius.

****

1982. What more appropriate day can there be to interview Mel Brooks than April Fools' Day?

As I set up my recording equipment, I go into my usual humorous shtick to break the ice. Mel really likes my routine and tells me I'm uniquely funny. I have an ulterior motive. I explain that I've already dabbled in stand-up comedy. He says I'd be great at it. He's completely supportive, and not condescending in any way. It's obvious he means what he says. I'm beaming.

****

Midway through the interview, Mel says something that floors me. He tells me that he executive-produced the movie *The Elephant Man*, which I know as a deeply serious drama about a severely deformed man in London during the late 1800s. But Mel explains he intentionally remained uncredited as executive producer for fear that anyone seeing his name attached to the movie would expect it to be a comedy. He explains that he doesn't want to be pigeon-holed … that comedy isn't the only thing for which he wants to be known. It instantly gets me thinking.

****

Maybe I was wrong. I thought the interview had gone well. Why then was Mel Brooks chasing me down the stairs like a madman?

When he caught up to me, I noticed something in his hands. He said, "I want you to have this," as he presented me with a *History of the World, Part I* T-shirt. "And when you do stand-up, I want you to let me know. I want to come see you."

One of the all-time Kings of Comedy chased me down the stairs just to tell me he wants to come see me the next time I do stand-up. Could there be a higher compliment?

But it was already too late.

Once Mel told me he didn't want to be pigeon-holed, that comedy wasn't the only thing he wanted to be known for, my mind was changed instantly. My comedy was extremely sick comedy before sick comedy became the rage. I reasoned that if I became known as a sick comedian, I'd be pigeon-holed for life. And there were so many other serious things that I had planned for my future.

Mel Brooks had been so incredibly supportive, and I will always treasure his encouragement. But I knew at that moment I would never do stand-up again.

Today, I look back at that decision and regret that it was one of the great blunders of my life.

Chapter 39

My favorite live band of all time

It's Groundhog Day. You've got one band to see live every day for the rest of your life. What band would it be?

Some might say Bruce Springsteen & the E Street Band. They give 110% every night. A truly great show. But they're not my Groundhog Day band.

Others might say Earth, Wind & Fire. They put on an incredible live performance. They're close. But there's one band I could see play every day, and it's one you've probably never even heard of.

****

On January 18, 1982, I had the pleasure of interviewing Chubby Checker, my childhood musical idol. One month after the interview, MCA Records invited me to Chubby's show at the Country Club in Reseda, California. I couldn't refuse the invitation. I just had to see my boyhood hero, especially since he'd been such a nice and humble guy in the interview.

February 17, 1982

I arrived at the Country Club early enough to see the opening act, a group called Jack Mack & the Heart Attack. There'd been a lot of music industry buzz surrounding the band, but I knew nothing about them. As it turned out, the buzz was totally justified.

They were a white soul group … a horn band to rival any live R&B act I'd ever seen. I'm a sucker for bands with tight horn sections, Hammond B3 organs and soulful singers. It takes a lot for an opening act to hold my attention, but right away, this group had me dancing in my seat.

Then my producer, Lynnsey Guerrero, leaned excitedly across the table and asked me, "Do you know who the singer is? That's Max Gronenthal!" I was stunned. I'd interviewed Max in 1979, as a favor to Chrysalis Records, when he was a solo artist. The interview was for Max's first solo album, and the label had such little regard for him, they set us up to do the interview in their mail room. Most interviews were held in cushy conference rooms or hotel suites, not frickin' mail rooms. With little support from Chrysalis, the record went nowhere.

But that night at the Country Club, Max was absolutely amazing. And Jack Mack & the Heart Attack were on it. They out-Blues-Brothered the Blues Brothers Band. And the audience went wild. Poor Chubby. He had to follow this juggernaut. My idol, the top bill, was relegated to second fiddle. That night Chubby Checker was an afterthought. I can't even remember his set.

I wasn't the only one who was blown away by Jack Mack & the Heart Attack. The Eagles' Glenn Frey was such a fan that he produced and provided vocals on various cuts on their *Cardiac Party* LP. Max Gronenthal wrote or co-wrote the entire album.

The group's publicist was a friend of mine, Bunny Wright, whose boyfriend, John Paruolo, played Hammond B3 in the band. Bunny would call me whenever Jack Mack played locally in LA, and I jumped at the opportunity to see them over and over again.

One Brain Cell Left

My favorite venue to see them play was the legendary Palomino Club in North Hollywood. It only sat a few hundred people, so you were lucky if you got a seat to see the superstars who played there. George Harrison, Neil Young, Johnny Cash, The Pretenders, Linda Ronstadt, as far back as Patsy Cline … the stars all played there when they wanted to escape the larger, impersonal concert halls. Clint Eastwood's *Every Which Way But Loose* and *Any Which Way You Can* were both filmed there. The place reeked of entertainment history.

And when Jack Mack played there, the place just rocked. It was loud and raw and intimate, all at the same time. And you just couldn't sit still.

Band members have come and gone, but the band still plays and releases recordings to this day. And they sound as great as ever.

Max Gronenthal was one of the ones that left Jack Mack. Under his stage name, Max Carl, he became lead vocalist for .38 Special and then Grand Funk Railroad. Despite little respect from Chrysalis Records, Max has been inducted into three states' Music Halls of Fame … Nebraska, Kansas and Georgia, the latter as a member of .38 Special.

New Orleans' Mark Campbell is the current, soulfully powerful lead singer for Jack Mack. Think back to Michael J. Fox singing "Johnny B. Goode" in the 1985 movie, *Back to the Future*. You probably know that Michael didn't really sing the song. But you probably don't know that he was lip-synching to Mark Campbell's voice. The movie's producers didn't want anyone to know that it wasn't Michael, so Mark never got screen credit. But he did get residuals and a Gold Record.

You should check out Mark Campbell and Jack Mack's tribute to the greatest soul singers of all-time, called "Soul Man."

https://youtu.be/o7dbQRi1HUw

When Groundhog Day rolls around … again … and again … and again, I know who I want there playing for me. And, no, it won't be Bill Murray. It'll be a band that you've probably never even heard of. "The Hardest Working Band in Soul Business."

Chapter 40

I'll ask Fred and Wilma. They'll know.

I'm a dinosaur. A total fossil.

I'm so out of touch that this entire book was typed on a laptop that runs Windows Vista. I gave up my Smartphone for an old school flip phone a while ago, which didn't matter, because the Smartphone was smarter than I was anyway. I've never owned a tablet. I've never used social media. No Facebook. No Instagram. No Twitter. No Tumblr. I missed the Myspace era entirely.

When I left Westwood One in 1990, I dropped out completely. From going to every screening for every movie that came out and listening to every new artist and new album, I went to ground zero. No movies or music. I'm like a cicada that's been underground for 17 years.

I'm completely old school with anything pop culture. It's not that I think old school is better. It's not that I think today's music sucks. I just haven't been exposed to anything new in a quarter century.

I don't have cable television, or DISH or DirecTV. The only newer TV series I've seen in the last 15 years were *Psych* and *30 Rock*. I haven't been to a rock concert since the early '90s. I haven't read a book in 25 years. Except for this one.

I'd make for a perfect scientific experiment. "What do you think doctor? We found him frozen in the Arctic. He's been on ice since before the Clinton administration. We better ease him back into society. It might be too much of a shock for him." I'm like Brendan Fraser in *Encino Man*. Or for that matter, like Brendan Fraser in *Blast from the Past*.

I've been to movie theaters to see just two movies in the last 25 years, one in Hawaii and one in Palm Springs.

I haven't stayed up late to watch *Saturday Night Live* since the Eddie Murphy and Joe Piscopo era.

I don't know which show Ed McMahon hosts: *American Idol* or *Dancing with the Stars*.

I've never seen Taylor Swift perform ... or Justin Bieber ... or Ariana Grande.

I wouldn't know the difference between any of those people whose names start with 'K' that are related to the Kardashian guy from the OJ trial.

I wouldn't know *Real Housewives* from *Sister Wives*, *Duck Dynasty* from the Duggars.

Maybe it's time for me to catch up. But where would I start? I'll ask Fred and Wilma. They'll know.

Chapter 41

The Top 10 questions that I'm asked

That's me with the long curly hair and cool skinny tie. Carol Kleinman (C.) and Mike Reynolds (R.) were two of my Westwood One Los Angeles reporters. I also oversaw interviewers in London, New York, Washington, DC and Nashville.

Credit: Westwood One/Billboard Magazine

1. How did you decide which celebrities to interview?

If you've ever watched a late night talk show, you've seen actors pitching their latest movies and authors pitching their latest novels. My situation wasn't much different. A movie studio would contact me in advance of a release asking if I would interview its stars. For example, in 1984, Twentieth Century Fox called to see if I was interested in interviewing Michael Douglas, Kathleen Turner and Danny DeVito for a new movie called *Romancing the Stone*. My answer was, "Of course." Who wouldn't want to interview them? Westwood One aired the interviews nationally in conjunction with the movie's premiere.

It was the same with authors and the release of their books. It was a win-win for everyone. The book publisher received free publicity nationwide, and Westwood One would be on the cutting edge of pop culture.

With music, it was a bit different. I had to be much more proactive. *Billboard's* music charts usually reflected record sales, but sales generally followed radio airplay. If I waited for songs to reach *Billboard's* Top Ten, I might be too late. The song might no longer be getting airplay. So my "bible" was the weekly *Radio & Records* industry newspaper. It tracked what songs radio stations were playing. Each week I would scour the various chart formats (e.g., pop, rock, R&B, country) to see what artists and songs were just starting to get airplay on leading radio stations nationwide. I would contact the record companies early on to request interviews. An artist's success on the *Radio & Records* charts usually dictated which musicians I'd pursue.

2. How did you get the interviews?

Once I decided which artists I'd pursue, I usually called the record companies' publicity departments to arrange an interview. Often managers or record companies would hire outside publicity firms to handle their artists' PR, so I'd also call independent publicists on a daily basis. Once in a while I would go directly to the managers, but usually I went through the artists' publicists.

In 1978, when I first started doing music interviews for Record Report, I had to really push to get known by the PR departments. It could take weeks before I'd get a returned call, if one came at all. But I was very persistent. I'd leave a message and wait two days. If I got no response, I'd call again. I didn't want to call every day for fear that I'd piss off the publicist. But I'd call every two days until I got the publicist on the phone. I memorized the phone numbers of all the record companies' publicity departments, so I could call them even when I was away from home or the office. It took months, but my persistence paid off. I became known by every music publicist in LA, and I often got the publicist on the phone on the first try.

I left the industry the first time shortly before Thanksgiving of 1979. When I surfaced at Westwood One in December of 1980, I had to start all over again. Many of the publicists that I'd worked with were gone, and few knew Westwood One. Again I had to be persistent, but eventually I again became known at every record company and music PR firm in Los Angeles, and most in New York and Nashville.

3. Where did you do the interviews?

The locations varied, but they included:

- Record companies (Madonna at Warner Bros. in Burbank, Michael Jackson at CBS Records in Century City, Janet Jackson at A&M Records in Hollywood);
- Publicists' offices (The Beach Boys, Doobie Brothers, Monty Python, Cheech & Chong);
- Hotels (Aerosmith at a Beverly Hills Hotel villa, Harrison Ford and Sean Connery at the Bel-Air Hotel, Duran Duran at the Chateau Marmont, AC/DC at the Sunset Marquis);
- Management company offices (Tina Turner, Alice Cooper, Rick James);
- Celebrities' homes (Quincy Jones, Kurt Russell, Joe Namath, Ray Bolger, Johnny Mathis, Gladys Knight, Lionel Richie);
- The cab of a pickup truck (Motorsports Hall of Fame drag racer Shirley Muldowney);
- The Record Report office (the three remaining Doors, Ted Lange of *The Love Boat*);
- The Westwood One office (Steve Wozniak, Spinal Tap, Eddie Munster);
- Television studios (Jay Leno, Dick Clark, Harry Chapin);
- Recording studios (REO Speedwagon, Randy Newman);

- A band's tour bus (INXS);
- Movie sets (Eddie Murphy);
- Restaurants (Kenny Rogers);
- Backstage (Paul McCartney, Wayne Newton);
- Home recording studios (Barry White);
- An airplane hangar (Francis Gary Powers);
- Locker rooms (Kareem Abdul-Jabbar);
- The celebrities' own offices (Mel Brooks, Steve Allen, George Burns);
- Movie studio offices (Carl Reiner, Dan Aykroyd);
- Radio stations (Arnold Schwarzenegger).

4. How long did the interviews last?

Usually the interviews were scheduled for one hour. I often interviewed the same artists multiple times, when an hour wasn't enough or when a new single was released.

5. How long in advance did you set up the interviews?

Many of the artists didn't live in the LA area, so I had to call two or three weeks ahead to ensure that I'd get them when they came to Southern California. Often I'd get the interview when the acts would come through on tour. Once in a while I'd get a call from a publicist for an interview that same day (Journey, Teddy Pendergrass), but that was rare.

Some took a lot longer. I contacted Arista Records nine months before Whitney Houston's first album was released, because I knew she was going to be a star. I'd heard a duet she did with Teddy Pendergrass on his comeback album following the car accident that left him paralyzed. I asked Shep Gordon, Teddy's manager, who the female singer was. He told me it was Cissy Houston's daughter, Whitney. I'd known of Cissy for years. I called Arista that day to put in my request for a Whitney interview. I had no idea it would take nine months or that it would be the only interview I'd ever get with her.

6. Where were you based?

I did most of my interviews in the LA area. Much of the time I worked from home. I could make my calls in private, and I could bang through them very quickly. I did much of my background research and listened to records at home before I left for the interviews. I also considered my "office" to be anywhere I could borrow a phone to make calls (record companies, hotels, etc.). This was long before we all had cell phones.

At Record Report in North Hollywood, Lynnsey Guerrero and I shared an office, but I rarely accomplished much there. We were too busy telling jokes to get much done, the kind of jokes that would get us arrested today.

I spent nearly 10 years working out of the Westwood One studios in the Los Angeles suburb of Culver City, across the street from the hotel where the Munchkins stayed during the filming of the *Wizard of Oz*.

7. Did you travel for the interviews?

While the bulk of my interviews were done in LA (Hollywood, Beverly Hills, Burbank, Century City, the Sunset Strip), I did travel outside of Southern California. Some of the areas included Las Vegas, Nashville, San Francisco, New York, Jamaica, Hungary, West Germany, Miami, Memphis, Lake Tahoe and Lake Shasta.

8. Do you have any of the interviews?

Unfortunately, I'm a pretty honest person. Record Report and Westwood One paid me for the exclusive rights to the interviews. So I turned in the cassettes and never made copies. I felt that was the right thing to do. I found out later that some of my reporters made copies, and one even resold them to Westwood One's competitors. My Jewish guilt would never have allowed me to do that.

9. Did you get any autographs?

To get the best possible interview, I needed to show the celebrities that I was their equal. I felt that if I asked for autographs, they would consider me their inferior or just a "fan." So the only autograph I got was from Mickey Mantle, and that was because my brother asked me to do it for him. Even then I had major reservations.

10. What technology did you use?

I used a radio-quality cassette recorder and a radio-quality handheld microphone, equipment that was readily available to the public. That was it. Simple, but effective.

My calendaring technology was state-of-the-art. Remember the old Rolodexes and the weekly AT-A-GLANCE appointment books? That was my technology. That was long before PC calendars. There were no Smartphones or tablets. I would handwrite the contact info on Rolodex cards and in the back of my appointment books. My follow-up calls were handwritten on half sheets of paper (one sheet for each day) that fit perfectly in the appointment books. If I didn't get to a call that day, I would handwrite it again on the ensuing day's sheet. I would have sheets for follow-up calls as much as two or three months ahead of time, so I wouldn't forget.

I still have all of my old Rolodexes and AT-A-GLANCE books. I wasn't sure why I was keeping them, but I just thought they might come in handy some day. The appointment books have been essential in writing this book. I was able look back and find when, where and with whom I conducted the vast majority of my interviews. Unfortunately, I didn't write every one down, so some are lost forever. I eventually built a computer database to store the details of more than 1600 of my interviews.

Chapter 42

Robin Williams committed suicide yesterday

August 12, 2014

I've cried a lot over the past 24 hours, but not for the reason you might think. Yes, I feel completely betrayed that we'll no longer have Robin's amazing talent. But my real reason is much more selfish.

I suffer from severe bipolar disorder, and the No. 1 cause of premature death for bipolars is suicide. I don't know if Robin ever admitted that he was mentally ill, but it was quite apparent to me just by watching him over the years. As soon as I read yesterday's headline, it was confirmed for me.

****

My psychiatrist was the one who told me the suicide rate among bipolars was much higher than the general population. She said it almost matter-of-factly, and I interpreted it as if she was giving me the green light to take my own life. It took me a while to realize what her real intent was. If I was aware that suicide was prevalent among bipolars, then I might recognize the symptoms of an episode early on, and that might keep me from ever trying to take my own life.

Several years earlier, after six months of deep depression, I had sunk to the point where I literally didn't care if I got run over by a bus. At least it would be over. Although I never considered suicide (I'm extremely squeamish and a chickenshit), I knew then that it was time to seek help.

I told my primary doctor about all the symptoms I'd been suffering. The bounce-off-the-wall highs. The zero-to-60 anger. The road rage. The desperate, despondent lows, including crying at Leave it to Beaver. The instantaneous mood swings in any and all directions.

"Son, you're bipolar," he said. "I can either recommend you to a psychiatrist, who'll put you on Lithium, or I can prescribe something right now." I said, "Doc, I need help right now."

That was it. No discussion of what bipolar disorder was. Just take this magic pill, and you'll be cured. Like antibiotics.

Wrong.

Little did I know that was just the start of a 10-year clinical depression. More doctors ... more meds to combat more symptoms.

One day I asked Marla what single word she would use to describe me. I figured "sweet," "intelligent," "funny." Her answer: "Tortured."

She and I were driving one day when Garbage's "Only Happy When It Rains" came on the radio. Without turning my head, I could sense Marla staring at me. We both knew Shirley Manson was singing about me.

****

Out of the blue, it happened. I felt this literal pop, like a bubble bursting in my head. Instantly I felt great. The cloud that surrounded me for a decade had lifted. I actually felt something foreign ... happiness.

I told the psychiatrist about the pop ... that I was miraculously cured. She had a sad look that spoke volumes ... a look that said, "Poor guy. He doesn't know there's no cure for BD." At that moment, I realized being bipolar was forever.

I went to another psychiatrist, who gave me a 500-question test. Based on the results, he diagnosed me as suffering from severe bipolar disorder, severe anxiety disorder, severe social anxiety disorder and moderate obsessive-compulsive disorder. When he read me his findings, it was like he was reading my diary. Everything he said was me. For 24 hours, I was absolutely overwhelmed and utterly crushed.

But a day later, I felt a sense of relief. At least I could put labels on all that I'd been experiencing. Yes, I was a nut case, but at least I wasn't a hypochondriac. What I was going through was real.

For the first time, I started to research bipolar disorder. For the first time, I could look back over my life and see how all of my bad decisions were fueled by BD. For the first time, I could rid myself of the guilt that those bad decisions caused.

Years after, but unfortunately too late, I realized that my deceased father had been bipolar, too. His constant anger finally had a tangible root. I suddenly had empathy for the misery that he endured because he went undiagnosed. I'm only sorry that I never had the chance to talk with him bipolar-to-bipolar. It may have made a difference in our strained relationship.

Early detection is the critical key to giving bipolars a chance at a somewhat normal life. I know that if I'd been diagnosed at an early age, I could have avoided the pain of so many terrible bipolar-influenced decisions.

Unfortunately, far too many mentally ill people like Robin Williams are unable to fend off that one final, irreversible decision. For many, living with mental illness is simply too painful.

Today, I'm completely open about my various mental illnesses. Yes, I often feel the stigma that society attaches to such disorders. But they're not my fault. I didn't cause them. They've been there my whole life.

I now know that it's cyclical. I spiral upwards for a brief period of time. Then I crash backwards. It's the nature of the beast. At least I recognize the symptoms more quickly.

In a perverse way, it's easier knowing that bipolar is forever.

Chapter 43

I'm no Belushi, but I've become Joe Cocker

Joe Cocker
Credit: Carl Lender/Wikimedia Commons

April 19, 1982

Awkward moments. We've all had our share. The toilet-paper-stuck-to-the-bottom-of-the-shoe moments. Whether you're telling others they have spinach in their teeth, or they're telling you, it's a lose-lose situation.

Meeting a celebrity for the first time before an interview is often a bit awkward. You have just minutes to break the ice. My M.O. as I was setting up my equipment was to break through the clumsy moments with really sick humor. Most entertainers loved it. It made them laugh, it put them in a fun place, and it set me apart from other interviewers. I had more than one artist say they wanted me doing stand-up to open for them on their tours, they liked my sick humor so much.

Then there was David Gates of the group Bread. I should have known by the syrupy songs he sang.

I started my shtick with Gates as soon as I entered the room. No response. More perverse humor. No response. The more sick comedy I tried, the less response I got, which made me try even harder. Absolutely nothing. Finally I gave up and started the interview, but by then it was too late. The awkwardness was too hard to overcome. I'd doomed the interview before it began.

It was only after the interview that I found out why. I told the record company publicist about my attempts at sick humor and how difficult the interview had been. She laughed and told me that Gates was extremely religious. Good thing she thought it was really funny. But I knew then that I should tone down my humor. Of course, I never did. Sick comedy was just my thing.

****

One Brain Cell Left

And then there was the late Joe Cocker and the most awkward moment I ever experienced during an interview. I'd been a fan of his since the early '70s. Amazing talent. Incredibly unique stage presence made even more unforgettable by John Belushi's parody of him on Saturday Night Live.

I was excited to get to interview Joe. I had no idea what to expect. Was his persona all an act? Or was it real? I'd soon find out.

Note the date: **April 19, 1982**

****

It turns out Joe's a really nice guy. Polite. Friendly. Soft-spoken. Almost shy. He's gone through a hard rock and roll life, but he's survived and thankful for the attention. "It's great to be here in 1981," he says. It's a little awkward (it's 1982, after all), but how many times have I mistakenly written the wrong year on a check? I don't mention it. We continue.

Another 10 minutes go by in the interview. Then he says it again. "It's great to be here in 1981." Unbelievably awkward. It's a toilet-paper-stuck-to-the-bottom-of-the-shoe moment. I really don't want to say anything, but I have to. This time I pause the tape and sheepishly say, "Joe, I've got to tell you, but it's 1982." The quizzical look on his face makes me cringe. He's completely perplexed, then utterly embarrassed. He's lived a hard, rock and roll life, and it's taken its toll. Poor Joe Cocker doesn't even know what year it is. It's indeed been a hard life.

I've told this story for more than three decades, and each time I've told it, I've felt sorry and embarrassed for him. Then one day recently, I realized that I'd become Joe Cocker. Bipolar disorder and its treatment have left me with just one brain cell. Six daily psych meds, including medical marijuana, mostly keep me from the frenzied highs and crushing lows of the disease. But they've left me so brain-dead that I have almost no memory whatsoever. I can't remember 99 percent of the interviews that I've done. I can't remember my thoughts midway through a sentence.

I'm no John Belushi, but I've become Joe Cocker. Sometimes I have to concentrate to remember what year it is.

****

My life hasn't always been pretty, but it's always been pretty interesting. I've interviewed mega-celebrities, superstar athletes and intriguing newsmakers. I've had Hall of Famers swear at me and flip me off. I've had a cop's gun pressed against my forehead, and I've had someone try to kill me. I've saved a couple of lives, too.

I've had tons of laughs, as well as tear-filled conversations with those I've met along the way. I've developed lifelong friendships and relationships with those I worked with during that manic snapshot in time. I've been naked, drunk and stupid and had stupid done to me. At times, it's been shocking and embarrassing. But it's also been interesting and entertaining.

And through it all, I've remained completely unknown worldwide.

Still, sometimes I wonder what my life would've been like if I had just one more brain cell. Then I realize it would've only been half as much fun.

Made in the USA
Columbia, SC
16 September 2020

20910037R00095